PRAISE FOR
RUNNING WITH PURPOSE

"Jim Weber is one of the great brand leaders of today. He has carefully shaped the Brooks experience to honor the legacy of running and Brooks customers. This is a definitive story of what can happen when you zero in on the essence of your customers' beliefs and then build a brand and culture of passion around that." **—TOD LEIWEKE,**
CEO, Seattle Kraken

"Jim's message will resonate with anyone, whether you run or not. His judgment, focus on sustainability and responsible sourcing, and efforts to foster a culture of fun in the workplace have led to some of the most impressive business results around. There is much to learn from this engaging read." **—SRI ZAHEER,**
Dean, Carlson School of Management,
University of Minnesota, and Board Chair,
Federal Reserve Bank of Minneapolis

"Whether you are an entrepreneur setting out with your first brick-and-mortar or running a global corporation, the learnings from Jim Weber's fascinating story will help any leader frame their strategy for success. Jim's tale of how he built Brooks to become the market leader among giants is an inspiring reminder that when you lead with heart and remain steadfast to even a lofty vision, there are no limits to what you can accomplish." **—KATHY DALBY,**
CEO, Pacers Running,
and Industry Leader

"Jim Weber's remarkable new book chronicles his amazing success story with Brooks Running, inspired by his authentic leadership and his crucible in overcoming a life-threatening bout with cancer. His openness and insights make *Running with Purpose* a must-read book for everyone." **—BILL GEORGE,**
Senior Fellow, Harvard Business School,
former Chair and CEO, Medtronic,
and author of *Discover Your True North*

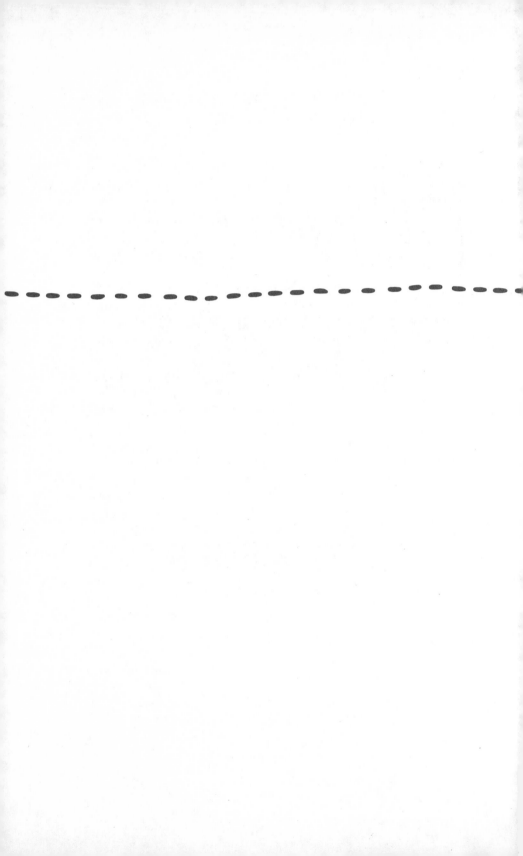

FOREWORD BY WARREN BUFFETT

RUNNING WITH PURPOSE

HOW BROOKS OUTPACED GOLIATH COMPETITORS TO LEAD THE PACK

JIM WEBER

CEO, BROOKS RUNNING COMPANY

HarperCollins
Leadership

AN IMPRINT OF HarperCollins

Published by HarperCollins Leadership,
an imprint of HarperCollins Focus LLC.

Any internet addresses, phone numbers, or company or product
information printed in this book are offered as a resource and are not
intended in any way to be or to imply an endorsement by
HarperCollins Leadership, nor does HarperCollins Leadership vouch
for the existence, content, or services of these sites, phone numbers,
companies, or products beyond the life of this book.

Book design by Aubrey Khan, Neuwirth & Associates, Inc.

ISBN 978-1-4002-3170-6 (eBook)
ISBN 978-1-4002-3168-3 (HC)

Library of Congress Cataloging-in-Publication Data
Library of Congress Cataloging-in-Publication
application has been submitted.

Printed in the United States of America
22 23 24 25 26 LSC 10 9 8 7 6 5 4 3 2 1

TO MARYELLEN

We did not know where our journey would lead,

but I am forever grateful to be walking,

running, and living it by your side.

CONTENTS

Foreword by Warren Buffett ix

Introduction xi

→ Part I

1. Stumbling Out of the Blocks 3
2. Picking Up the Pace 23
3. Pivot #1: Running Only 41
4. Becoming an Authentic Leader 59
5. Defining Moments: The Great Recession and an Earthquake in Running 73

→ Part II

6. Meeting the Oracle of Omaha 105
7. Pivot #2: Performance Is Timeless (We Zig When They Zag) 125
8. Finding Another Gear While Navigating Global Disruptions 143
9. Hitting a Wall: Fighting Cancer 163
10. Filling the "White Space" with Trust 179
11. On Your Left! Running Fast in a New Decade 193

Conclusion   203

Acknowledgments   205

Bibliography   209

Index   215

About the Author   223

FOREWORD

Jim Weber's career as a Berkshire Hathaway manager is unique.

Throughout my fifty-six-year tenure at Berkshire, the company has followed a dramatic hands-off style in its operations. Today, only twenty-five employees work for the parent company in headquarters, while three hundred sixty thousand go about their jobs in the many dozens of individually managed subsidiary businesses that Berkshire has purchased over the years. Our decentralization is extreme.

Among those many purchases was Fruit of the Loom, a Kentucky-based manufacturer of apparel, best known for men's underwear. Fruit is successful and well managed, employing about twenty-nine thousand people.

In 2012, Fruit owned several noncore operations, including Brooks Running Company, managed by Jim Weber. Brooks and, more particularly, Jim caught my eye. Jim would catch anyone's eye; he is a force.

I decided that Jim was simply too talented to not be running his own show, one that would report directly to Berkshire. My course was obvious: Fruit should transfer Brooks to Berkshire, and then Brooks should operate as a stand-alone business.

This decision—the only one of its kind ever made at Berkshire—has been a home run. Despite entrenched and able competitors, Jim has propelled Brooks forward to an extent far beyond my high expectations.

Jim loves running, loves runners, loves his associates, and loves his retailers. Daily he demonstrates that affection in his decision-making. He instinctively understands product design and branding. He will never settle for less than the best for all constituencies and constantly challenges himself.

His enthusiasm for running has been contagious with Berkshire shareholders. During our annual meeting weekend, thousands of attendees turn out for a Sunday-morning 5K. Prior to the event's pandemic-induced suspension, the crowd grew annually. I expect a new attendance record when an in-person meeting is resumed.

Jim's passionate story will inspire you just as it inspired me in 2012 to recognize that he would make Brooks a stand-alone star at Berkshire. I will recommend that all Berkshire managers, current and future, read this book.

— WARREN BUFFETT

INTRODUCTION

The push I needed to commit, sit down, and write a book came from Warren Buffett. In February 2020 (one month before the COVID-19–driven global shutdowns), I had just spent a few days in Atlanta taking in the 2020 Olympic Marathon Trials where the fastest marathoners in America would compete for a spot on Team USA for the upcoming Tokyo Games. I had recently started a dialogue with Warren to get his perspective on the broad-based erosion of trust in business, institutions, and leaders. I was trying to better understand its causes and context to more effectively respond to the expanding environmental, social, and governance (ESG) principles that I and every business leader was (and still are) being challenged to address. Warren invited me to Omaha for a Sunday morning breakfast meeting on my way home from that Atlanta trip, and we dove into a lively discussion on all things Brooks, the economy, and my leadership trust topic. As we closed out our morning conversation he added, "Brooks is a great story. You should write a book." Warren's prompt was not an entirely new idea for me.

In 2015, at age fifty-five, I took only my second extended work vacation ever. I'd taken off a day here and there but nothing longer than a week (I am not proud of that, by the way). Years prior, when Brooks was struggling and trying to retain talent, we created a sabbatical program where at 13.1 years of service, every employee was eligible for a paid four-week mini sabbatical. So there I was, on the longest-ever break since I started working in the family business at eight years old. I decided to go off the grid for the month and committed to write four hours every morning to chronicle my life journey. I also committed to learning to play guitar and after lessons and daily practice struggles, wisely chose to keep my day job. I ended up writing thirty thousand words and gave it the working title "Running Down a Dream." The end of my sabbatical also brought about the end of my daily writing routine as I instantly reengaged at work with renewed energy for the opportunity I saw for Brooks. And then came Warren's encouragement.

I believed to my core that the Brooks story as a brand, business, and "rags to riches" turnaround deserved to be told; a book had been in the back of my mind for a while. Others outside our industry had noticed our progress, too, as Brooks was the subject of a few business-school case studies, and I had often traveled back to the Tuck School at Dartmouth to bring alive lessons from the Brooks journey for MBA students.

In writing *Running with Purpose,* my first book, I had a few big questions to answer. The first was why write it? The answer for me was that I truly wanted to tell the world about the Brooks story. Through focus, creativity, and hard work, the Brooks team has created an exceptional company, and I want more people—especially runners—to know about the brand. After answering the why, there was the challenge to define what elements of Brooks's journey were relevant. Which story angles were most interesting and to whom?

First, Brooks is a great turnaround story. At ninety years old, the brand was refounded after a near bankruptcy and went on to not just survive but thrive in a highly competitive market. Brooks then navigated headwinds including the Great Recession, a few cycles of industry disruption, and a global pandemic with broad economic impact. We have embraced the necessity of intense focus, agility, and resilience, words that can almost ring as buzzwords as they are much easier to say than do.

Next, Brooks is a great David-and-Goliath, competitive strategy story. It is quite easy to name the leading platform players in any given industry—including athletic footwear and apparel—

and identify their logos. Earlier in my career I dreamed about working at a dominant platform company with network effects, recurring subscription revenue, and increasing returns as you scale, but my journey never took me there. When I started at Brooks, we were smaller than nine other companies in running; Nike was 153 times our size. We had to find ways to compete as a challenger brand and still deliver growth and financial results at the top quartile of our industry. It has not been a simple puzzle to solve, but it sure is rewarding when you win.

Another angle is Brooks's purpose-driven brand building story that, for over twenty years, has been anchored in shared values and an obsession with our target customer: runners. We have nurtured a culture that can attract and retain the talent needed to execute Brooks's unique brand positioning and strategy. We are committed to creating the best performance gear in the world, earning the runner's trust mile after mile, and then managing our business profitably to reinvest for growth. Brooks is a "built to last" brand in the making.

Then of course this book had to be about running as it is the market in which Brooks plays to win, let alone my own forty-year addiction to it. The largest category in sporting goods, running is a powerful, positive force for over one hundred fifty million people both as a sport and as an investment in themselves. At my current stage of life, I have begun to refer to my walks as "slow running," and Brooks's customer proposition extends to trail running and hiking as well. The invitation to keep moving is always there: Right foot, left foot—repeat!

Yet another storyline is leadership, specifically Brooks's dedication and commitment to helping managers at all levels develop into authentic leaders. We have evolved our leadership approach to drive a collaborative, connected, team-based culture that can execute at a high level. Brooks is known for its brand and products, but these are created by our people, so we put employees at the center of how we succeed. I generally don't mind publicly sharing our strategies as they could never be successfully executed by another company without the right team leading it every day.

Finally, I asked myself if there was an angle in this book to share my personal journey. Would that story have any takeaway value for the reader? I have found that as I get older, I know myself better and have come to believe that everyone is a product of their individual circumstances and journey. My early life experiences created a lot of hard wiring in me, and it took me about forty years to decode it and understand why I am who I am. If you are still learning, open minded, or generally curious, you might find useful lessons in my personal journey to become the best leader you can be.

In the end, I could not settle on one angle so *Running with Purpose* is a story about all of the above. I sincerely hope it has takeaway value for you at some level as life is too short and your time is too precious. At the very least, I hope you are inspired to run as it will make your day better!

Oh, and one more thing . . . like so many people, I love great music and the artists who create it. My life has a soundtrack starting with the music my mother loved and played in my childhood home including Johnny Cash, Roy Orbison, Elvis, and more. For many long runs since, I would create my perfect playlist to fit the moment. So for me, it only felt natural that I had a soundtrack for this book as I wrote it. If you want to add sonic context to your read of *Running with Purpose*, below is a start to a playlist. Access these songs on your vinyl albums, 8-track tapes, cassette tapes, CDs, or, of course, your favorite streaming service:

Chapter 1
Stumbling Out of the Blocks
- Bob Dylan, "Tangled up in Blue"
- Led Zeppelin, "Kashmir"

Chapter 2
Picking Up the Pace
- Led Zeppelin, "Ramble On"

Chapter 3
Pivot #1: Running Only
- Tom Petty and the Heartbreakers, "Running Down a Dream"

Chapter 4
Becoming an Authentic Leader
- Bob Dylan, "My Back Pages"

Chapter 5
Defining Moments:
The Great Recession and an Earthquake in Running
- R.E.M., "It's the End of the World as We Know It (And I Feel Fine)"

Chapter 6
Meeting the Oracle of Omaha
- Bob Dylan, "It's Alright, Ma (I'm Only Bleeding)"
- Pink Floyd, "Money"

Chapter 7
Pivot #2: Performance Is Timeless
(We Zig When They Zag)
- R.E.M., "Stand"

Chapter 8
Finding Another Gear While
Navigating Global Disruptions
- Talking Heads, "Once in a Lifetime"

Chapter 9
Hitting a Wall: Fighting Cancer
- John Mayer, "Say"
- Gregory Alan Isakov, "Second Chances"

Chapter 10
Filling the "White Space" with Trust
- Joni Mitchell, "Big Yellow Taxi"
- Bob Dylan, "The Times They Are a-Changin'," "Chimes of Freedom"

Chapter 11
On Your Left! Running Fast in a New Decade
- Macklemore and Ryan Lewis, "Can't Hold Us"
- Jakob Dylan, "Something Good This Way Comes"

PART I

CHAPTER 1

Stumbling Out of the Blocks

T'S 1963, I AM THREE YEARS OLD, and I am running. My mom, brothers, sisters, aunts, and cousins are having a backyard picnic.

I am just running.

I was one of those kids who was always inside his own head, presenting myself as shy and introverted. I'd run around that backyard, trying to soak it all in. I was one of six kids, all born within eight years of one another, in an extended family with thirty-seven cousins, all within six miles. Age-wise, I was kind of in the middle, a tweener. The truth is I never felt that I fit in. I do not recall a happy, settled childhood. Looking back, I may have been running around in circles in that backyard, but within a few years there would be days when I would want to run away.

We lived in the working-class suburb of North St. Paul, Minnesota, twenty minutes from Minneapolis and twenty minutes from the Saint Croix River on the Wisconsin border. To many, that's the middle of nowhere. To me, it's home.

My dad built our small house just before I was born. What I remember most is that it had a red brick fireplace, a swing set, and a sandbox out in the backyard. I slept in a basement bedroom with my two brothers. My mom was reliably a glass-half-full person with a welcoming, empathetic presence and a ready smile for everyone in her life.

Dad was the opposite. I could sense his mood, which often seemed stressed, bitter, and unhappy. Though he was most often a glass-half-empty kind of guy, growing up I saw his glass filled with Canadian whiskey and soda. He started around 9:00 a.m., refilled it throughout the day, and always had one at dinnertime. This was his daily routine. Alcohol was always in his system. My mom and dad didn't exactly balance each other out. I witnessed two clearly distinct approaches to engaging people and the energy you create from the attitude you carry in daily life.

The Weber home was chaotic, to say the least. Uncertainty, negativity, stress, and fear shaped my early life. I mostly kept to myself—thinking, worrying, imagining, and dreaming. It didn't help that I was a bed-wetter. This was a painful and embarrassing issue for me as a child. I would wake up many mornings soaking wet. My mom would have to scramble to clean my sheets, dry out the bed, and somehow make me presentable for school. This was on top of caring for my two younger sisters, creating six custom lunches (each with our names lovingly written on the front), and getting us all out the door. My lunch, every day, consisted of Tastee Bakery white bread, Skippy and Welch's PB&J, Old Dutch chips, and homemade chocolate chip or peanut butter cookies. But getting off to the right start didn't always happen.

One morning in second grade, my teacher was in the middle of a lesson for first period when she paused, stepped back, and asked if someone in the room had wet their pants. Fear and shame ran down my spine. I knew I was the guilty one. The odor from the previous night lingered. I did not raise my hand. Frozen in place, I was terrified she was going to walk the aisles and call me out in front of the class. Maybe everyone already knew it was me. I had no idea. I never saw a doctor about it. But the Mayo Clinic, just south of our home, lists stress and anxiety as the number-one risk factor for chronic childhood bed-wetting.

During my childhood, I can't remember seeing my dad happy (unless he had had too much to drink), but I later learned that had not always been the case. A year before he died at age eighty-four, he and my mom shared their stories over dinner with just me. This was to be our first real conversation, ever.

He had played football in high school, hunted, and fished with his dad. After graduation, he enrolled at the College of St. Thomas in St. Paul with the idea of becoming an engineer. He loved to build things and had worked on construction crews as a kid. Building things was clearly his happy place. Ultimately, though, college was not a fit. Dad went back to construction, running crews until he was drafted to join the Army during the Korean War. Fortunately, his knowledge of drafting and engineering was just enough to keep him out of harm's way on a bridge-building crew. After a two-year stint in the Army, he briefly returned to construction, but then his father died unexpectedly. We suspected regular consumption of alcohol was a contributing factor.

→ Family Business

Beginning in the 1940s, my grandfather ran Weber's Supper Club, a twelve-lane bowling alley, bar, nightclub, and restaurant. The business was successful, and just as they took on debt to expand into a brand-new building, my grandfather died. My grandmother asked my dad to come into the business, so he left his construction business at age twenty-three. The club was a daily struggle both for my dad and my grandmother. For the next forty years, it was his entire life. Running a bar, of course, made alcohol available to him all day, every day. I remember being there one morning doing my job rolling quarters, dimes, and nickels from the vending machines to be brought to the bank, when a customer came into the bar at 9:00 a.m. and said, "Good morning all!"

My dad didn't respond, but my grandmother looked up with a scowl and asked bitterly, "What's good about it?" The negativity of that response shook me then, and still does. Life seemed too short to be that sad, angry, or bitter, especially at the start of the day.

My mother and her side of the family, the Schaefers, were social, happy, welcoming, and positive people. I have a lot of Weber in my persona, but I always wanted to be happy and connected to people like my grandmother on the Schaefer side. I wanted to draw people to me, not push them away. Years later, as the CEO of Brooks, we all took the Insights Discovery test: blue for precise and focused; red for decisive and assertive; green for connected and caring; yellow for outgoing and engaging. I've been a yellow "wannabe" my entire life.

In the Myers-Briggs world, I'm an introvert who wants to be an extrovert. A work forever in progress, I remind myself every day that attitude is a choice, and open, optimistic, positive people are magnetic to others.

By age ten, I had begun to figure out a few things about myself. I had started skating and playing hockey on our street and the nearby ponds and rinks with cousins and friends from school and the neighborhood. I'd go to their homes afterward, in part to avoid my dad's unpredictability. That was when I began to notice a distinct difference between the relaxed, calm, happy, and engaging people at their homes, and the gray clouds and need to walk on eggshells at mine.

I ended up building my own world. Outside of sports, I spent a lot of time alone. I especially loved to take things apart and build new things in my dad's garage workshop. I had chemistry sets, erector sets, Legos, and the like. I worked on my bike. Often I went to the library to take out books on electronics. I built my own crystal radio and experimented with light circuits. I blew up many light bulbs plugging them into 120-volt sockets. Later, my brother and I would rebuild his 1967 Chevrolet Bel Air into our version of a cool streetcar, and I would build tower speakers for my stereo from handcrafted, solid oak cabinets to wiring woofers, crossovers, and tweeters that could play Led Zeppelin's "Kashmir" very loud. I loved understanding how things worked. This was a key ingredient in becoming an ad-mirer and connoisseur of great product design.

In seventh grade I was fortunate to have a teacher who chal-lenged me to learn from others and dream about my future. My English class was taught by Mrs. McGrath. She handed out daily assignments on the "Thought for the Day" that exposed us to great authors, philosophers, or artists and had us review-ing their genre and their greatest works. Then she challenged us with a paper that ended up giving me the focus and the nudge I needed. Mrs. McGrath asked us to write an essay on five different career scenarios for ourselves. Of course, like any self-respecting Minnesota kid, I picked "professional hockey player." I wrote about a hockey hero, Bobby Hull, who de-scribed how he got bored between practices and games, so I wrote that I'd also need a "sideline," perhaps a small business.

In addition to hockey player, I chose business manager, neu-rosurgeon, research scientist, and stockbroker. In Mr. Fulton's seventh-grade math class, we did stock-picking exercises and tracked the stocks' performances over time. I picked Arrow Electric and began to dream of becoming president of a com-pany like that. My dad's brother was the president of a major construction company. In fact, his company built the St. Paul Civic Center, a 16,000-seat arena that hosted the World Hockey Association's Minnesota Fighting Saints and every state high school hockey tournament. Several of my friends' parents who ran successful businesses seemed happy and certainly were not struggling. I had the inkling that I wanted to be like them.

Thanks to those middle school English and math classes, I had a clear goal to add to my hockey dreams. I would get an MBA and one day become president of a company.

Still, there was my total immersion in hockey.

→ Hockey Dreams

Hockey is a fast and physical game, and it also requires finesse, precision, skill, power, synchronistic team play, and fluidity. I first learned to skate on a postage-stamp-sized rink in a neighbor's yard. Eventually, I could seemingly skate forever over interlacing ponds and lakes. Minnesotans are fond of bragging that they can shoot the puck a mile. I know this from experience: The first hard freeze before snow is a slice of heaven for a skater. I've had to retrieve errant pucks that were driven by a slap shot to the other side of a lake.

In winter, everyone I knew skated on the ponds and local rinks. Youth Hockey was wildly popular. My goal became to go to Hill-Murray School, a local Catholic high school known for its hockey dynasty. My plan was to make the hockey team and then compete in the three-day, televised state championship at the St. Paul Civic Center. I dreamed of playing in the University of Minnesota Gopher hockey program, the Minnesota North Stars of the NHL, and, naturally, Team USA in the Olympics.

For me, hockey became an obsession. I put everything I had into it. I played on squirt, pee-wee, bantam, plus school teams, often on premier traveling teams and always in summer leagues. My mom drove me to multiple practices every week, some at 6:00 a.m. If she couldn't, I walked nearly a mile with my gear to Polar Arena on dark winter days or hitched a ride to games with teammates. I was big for my age and started as goalie but transitioned to other positions, eventually finding my spot as left wing.

I fixated on one player in particular who came out of North St. Paul. He went on to have a great high school career and played for the Gophers. He moved effortlessly up and down the ice. With a single flick of his wrist, he could rifle the puck into the upper corner of the net. It didn't matter whether he was off balance or moving at speed.

I spent hours in my garage trying to master that snapshot. I signed up for every summer league and continued to work on my stick handling to make sure I didn't leave anything on the ice. I ended up with a decent shot, but despite the hours I still couldn't deliver it at speed and off balance like he could.

All my siblings attended public school, but I was determined to talk my parents into letting me go to Hill-Murray. I knew family finances were strained, so I put in many hours at Weber's Supper Club mopping floors, cleaning bathrooms, and working the bowling counter. I also got on a commercial roofing crew in the summer to fund most of my tuition. At Hill-Murray, I signed up for football, hockey, and track. Since my dad was six feet two, I assumed I'd continue to grow. As it turned out, my mother's genes prevailed, and by age fourteen I was fully grown at five feet eight. In team photos, I went from being the tallest kid in the back row to sitting in front. As others kept growing, I was getting comparatively slower each year. In running terms, I didn't have a cadence issue; I had a stride-length issue.

At Hill-Murray, many of the great hockey players made varsity their freshman year and played all four years. That was my goal. And because I was so fixated on hockey, everything was on the line at that point in my life. To qualify for the later tryouts held on the ice, I first needed to run a sub-six mile on the track. Check. Then I made two of the three cuts when we got on the ice. But when the varsity list was posted, my name was not on it. My heart sank. It is hard to express how catastrophic that was at the time.

I went on to a good year on the junior varsity team and after just three games at the start of my sophomore year I was called up to varsity. My NHL dreams were intact. The school was a powerhouse in hockey. More than twelve teammates went on to Division 1 college hockey. The goalie was Steve Janaszak, who became the backup goalie to Jim Craig on the 1980 "Miracle on Ice" Olympic team. My line mate was Chris Pryor who eventually played in the NHL. I played on a regular shift, typically on third line, for the next three years at Hill-Murray. Each year our aim was to qualify for the state tournament and its enormous audience. It was the most thrilling experience of my life at that time. It seemed like everyone in the state was focused on the teams and players in this high school tournament. If I could distinguish myself as a player on one of the best teams in the state, I would have achieved something.

Each year before the state tournament, we had a team meeting in somebody's house to prepare mentally for the tournament. Sitting there during my senior year in a large circle, we were each asked to share our thoughts on the opportunity ahead. Given that this was my third state tournament without a championship and my last shot at getting one, I made a plea to everyone to set their minds on winning the championship trophy. Hill-Murray had won plenty of section titles. In previous state tournaments, we went home with third place or the Consolation Trophy. I wanted to win state. My mindset then would prove useful later in life: Winning begins with a belief in its possibility, and if you have a ticket to the game, why not play to win?

The coach echoed my sentiment. It felt good to be out front, challenging our team to be the best. We made an impressive effort but were shut out 1–0 by a great goalie. As for my future sideline, at Hill-Murray I had become class president twice, attended Boys State, was on the student council, wrote for the student newspaper, landed a role in the musical *Hello, Dolly!*, and was beginning to love leadership.

I went on to play hockey at St. Cloud State University. In fact, I followed a girl, MaryEllen, who followed her brothers and sisters to St. Cloud. MaryEllen and I went to the same high school but never met until senior year. That fall she had made the hockey cheerleading squad, and when I saw her on the ice during pregame warmups she was hard to ignore. Coming up over the holidays was a girl-ask-guy dance called the Silver Bell Ball, and I decided it would be wonderful if MaryEllen asked me to go with her. I let my interest be known by asking a mutual friend to try to stir the idea in her mind. I marshaled the courage to approach MaryEllen, introduce myself at the school library when she was at the dictionary, and broke the ice with small talk. She called me a week later to ask me to the Silver Bell Ball, and after just a few dates we were steadies. She would become my best friend and a true soulmate. She was rock solid in her calm, happy demeanor and spiritual centeredness. Her family life, unlike mine, seemed connected and cohesive. Her father was a successful local business owner and yet was approachable and a natural listener full of wise advice. MaryEllen and I have now been together for more than four decades.

After that freshman year at St. Cloud, my hockey dreams were fading. I had stopped growing, was one of the smallest players on the ice, and had not gotten any faster. It was pretty clear to me I was hitting a ceiling on my skills.

I seriously revisited that seventh-grade paper and the need for a "sideline." I still wanted to run a company, and I needed an MBA. So, I shifted my aspirations and focus. I hung up the skates in competitive hockey, and transferred to the University of Minnesota, where I would earn my degree in business. Along the way I became a progressively stronger student, and once again began to devour assignments and work hard for a strong grade point average, high test scores, and the leadership experiences I would need to get admitted to a top MBA program. As I plotted a path to running a business, I still managed to have some extra time since I was no longer skating six days a week for eight months of the year.

→ Falling in Love . . . with Running

The day after I hung up the skates after playing competitive college hockey, it occurred to me I had to find something to replace it. I loved playing hockey. At the core of it was the physical experience of moving fast on the ice with a puck— sprinting, weaving, shooting, passing, and battling all the while. Hockey delivered a high calorie burn and a great sweat; after a tough practice or a game, I was often completely spent in the best way. It was an all-in workout for the body, which also fed my soul. I needed to find a new activity that allowed me to exert myself, get my heart rate up, and fill my innate desire to move. It was 1980, and at the time, the "jogging boom" was underway, so, I gave it a go. And thus began my love affair with running.

For the next forty years, I would run three to five days a week. I needed it like I needed air and water. I loved how convenient running was. I could fit it in whenever my work and family schedule allowed—morning, noon, or even late at night after the kids were in bed. It was always waiting there for me, just outside my front door. Sometimes after dinner when the boys were young, we would grab the dog and head out on what we called bike-runs—the boys pedaling alongside the dog and me as we ran through our neighborhood streets. Missing a run day was never great; missing two in a row was bad and affected how I showed up at work and at home. More than once in our crazy, stressful lives as young parents, my wife, MaryEllen, would opine, "You need a run," and I would head outside.

In my twenties and thirties, running was an obsession for me. While I had run in high school as a sprinter in track to train for hockey, I never really considered myself a "runner." But that would now change as I needed to run. Marathons were for the first time becoming "a thing"—open to anyone who wanted to tackle the challenge. In 1982, I signed up for the Twin Cities Marathon in October and decided to up my mileage to get in shape. I had no real plan and not a clue what I was getting into.

I pinned on a race bib to join 4,000 runners in the inaugural 1982 Twin Cities Marathon. As this was in pre-chip timing days, my postcard's printed results reflect a three-minute finish time inflation as it took me that long after the gun went off to reach the start. I of course had to preserve for posterity my true race run time of 3 hours and 31 minutes.
Courtesy of Jim Weber

I always ran alone and had never talked with anyone who completed a marathon, nor did I consult a coach. I maxed my training on a twenty-miler, and it actually felt pretty good. Though I toed the start line with confidence, the race experience for me met the cliché of hitting the wall at mile twenty. Like my training, the first twenty miles were solid as I hit a seven-minute-mile pace and gained on other runners both up and down hills with my hockey legs. But that all changed as I came up the gradual hill from the Mississippi River to the last six miles coming into St. Paul. My body fell apart with my legs and feet in pain and no longer wanting to move. I clocked over eleven-minute miles for the rest of the race, finishing at three hours and thirty-one minutes. I was exhausted in a good way but humbled by the mental challenges of those last six miles, wishing the path from Marathon to Athens in Greece had been closer to 20 miles, not 26.2.

My favorite feature in *Runner's World* magazine was the "Rave Run" spread, serving up picturesque places around the world to run. Each month when my issue arrived, I quickly flipped through the pages in anticipation of where the "Rave Run" would take me. The images were powerful—I nearly felt transported as I longed to run in the landscapes pictured. I loved running in iconic, beautiful places. At the University of Minnesota, I would run the trails alongside the Mississippi River and into the neighborhoods of Summit Avenue in St. Paul. When I traveled, I would get a local map from the hotel front desk to discover the best trails in a new city. This is how I found myself running in New York City's Central Park on two inches of fresh snow, through the streets of Paris at sunrise on a summer morning, in Moscow's Red Square in the fall, and on Lady Bird Lake Trail in Austin, Texas, before or after days of meetings. Near my home is Bridle Trails State Park, where I run through a forest of second-growth cedar and fir trees leading to a grove of a few old-growth giants I visit whenever I can.

Running truly became meditation time for me. Mile after mile, I processed the biggest questions or challenges at work and in life that kept me awake at night. There were times my mind was so engaged as I ran that I would look up and not know exactly where I was, forcing me to check the street signs to get my bearings. On many of my birthdays, I put together a music mix—often anchored by deep tracks from Bob Dylan—and treated myself to a six-mile Zen run. Running for me was a gift.

→ Building My Credentials for Business Leadership

My first business turnaround came in those years at the University of Minnesota. I was elected president of the Sigma Nu Fraternity, a campus organization that had seen better days. Frat life can be a mixed bag, but for me it was a great way to make an enormous campus more manageable. We grew membership by 35 percent and raised money to make needed repairs to the fraternity house.

Another highlight at Minnesota came in the last quarter in 1982 in the MGMT 5101 advanced topics course on leadership. It featured different CEOs from the best companies in Minnesota at that time, including 3M, Target, Cray Research, Marvin Windows, and others. The course was taught by Wheelock Whitney, the former CEO of Dain Bosworth (now RBC Wealth Management) who had once run for governor of Minnesota.

Wheelock was super smart and insightful, but oh so human. His manner was gracious, generous, unpretentious, and inclusive. As students, we were invited to his home where he played guitar and sang songs around the campfire. He was the closest thing to a Renaissance man I had met at that time.

I'll never forget his closing speech on the course. In the end he made it clear that to be an effective leader, you need to have good judgment. I internalized that leadership truth as a personal challenge to myself. A leader needs to be right, at least about the big things. "Good judgment" would serve me well in my future.

The year MaryEllen and I graduated from the University of Minnesota and were married—1982—was one of the toughest job markets since the end of World War II. The country was in a deep recession, triggered by a tight monetary policy that attempted to fight mounting inflation. Unemployment reached 11 percent that year, inflation was rampant, and interest rates soared with the prime rate reaching a record 21 percent, creating the worst economic conditions since the Great Depression.

I was unsure whether to pursue sales, finance, or operations. The one thing I did know for certain was that I didn't want to be in a family restaurant business. I had no interest in being chained to failure or family conflict. I wanted to be in a real corporation with professional people and a career path that would lead me ideally to the opportunity to be president. In a competitive lottery system for interview slots, I ended up getting interviews with both major banks in the area, Norwest Bank and US Bank. I got offers from both banks and ultimately accepted the offer from Norwest, the largest bank in the Ninth Federal Reserve District.

Norwest, which was headquartered in Minneapolis and later merged with Wells Fargo, was an amazing experience, a crash course in learning about businesses through hands-on financial analysis necessary to assess creditworthiness for lending. I had a front-row seat on the corporate culture and a great deal of frontline client interaction. Picture a twenty-three-year-old loan officer responsible for lending money to clients the age of my parents and grandparents. I was lending money to, and trying to collect loans from, a wide variety of companies ranging from a hat and cap textile manufacturer to a used wig retailer to a medical products manufacturer and a wool sweater company. Before long, I knew I wanted to be on the company side of the conference table, inside a brand. As a young banker, I found working with company owners and CFOs inspiring. We were providing loans to make cool things happen in their businesses, and I was curious about their strategies and execution. It looked like a lot more fun than extending and collecting loans.

I began to plot my strategy to get into a top MBA program, which I believed was a critical step to being seen as leadership material. In my first year at the bank, I met Susan Cruess, who was a graduate of the Tuck School of Business at Dartmouth. She was adamant that I apply to Tuck, so I did, and she put in a good word for me with admissions. In an almost-replay from missing the varsity team at Hill-Murray, Tuck deferred a decision on my application to the final period, but then I finally got one of the most important letters of my career—acceptance to Tuck.

Tuck was a huge investment that I would largely fund with student loans. It was also a big move for our family, putting immense stress on us as new parents, particularly MaryEllen. It was clear I needed to make the most of it. MaryEllen and I had arrived at Tuck with our one-year-old son, Michael, and would leave with our second, Joel. We were quite aware that our social experience at Tuck was very different than if I had been single or if we did not have children. We weren't having the same social experiences as others. While I would join Friday night "Tuck Tails" with my classmates for one beer, from there it was home to be with my family. Although we often missed out on socializing, we never regretted our situation as we made great friends in the married community at Tuck. The experience was a huge part of our journey as a family.

The first year at Tuck was amazing and intense. Graduate school brings a whole different level of work and stress. The amount of reading, case preparation, group work, and projects for the term forces you to make decisions about priorities. It has a boot-camp–like pace with a fire hose of work coming at you that exceeds the hours in a day. This is particularly the case if you have an interest in any activities outside of the classroom, from sports to fitness to family. In the mid-1980s, I believe Tuck was unique in how team-oriented the culture and program were. We worked the cases in groups of four to five people for several hours every afternoon and evening. Once in class, the professors were fantastically skilled in creating a turbocharged learning environment.

To this day, some of the professors at Tuck are among the most insightful businesspeople I've ever been around. They teach you how to think like an investor or a CEO; they arm you with the mindset and tools to frame and solve any business problem that might come your way. It was foundational for me.

→ A Business Analyst with New Tools

At the time, the Apple Macintosh had just launched, and the PC (personal computer) era was underway. Earlier at Norwest Bank, our division got the first IBM PC with VisiCalc loaded on it. I grabbed it and became the first banker at Norwest to build "paperless" spreadsheets to drive analysis on historical financial statements and projections and ratio analysis around credit capacity. We had all been trained to "spread" the numbers on green columnar pads with pencil and eraser. It was great training to truly understand and internalize the numbers. But with VisiCalc, you could run scenario after scenario in minutes versus hours and never touch an eraser.

I used my PC to model revenue in detail, seeing through the dollars into circulation, response rates, and advertising dollar scenarios. For me, it was the start of not just looking at an income statement but looking through it to see that revenue and gross margin actually reflected customers' buying behaviors and their willingness to pay certain prices. I also built a model for Weber's

Supper Club that made it clear they needed to fill the bowling leagues to stem losses. But that was easier said than done.

At Tuck, we were one of the first PC-powered MBA classes. We all ordered our own computers. I ordered a brand-new IBM PC base-level machine. It was an 8086 with dual floppy disk drives, a Princeton amber monitor, and an OKI Data dot matrix printer that sounded like an eggbeater. We were the first generation of analysts trained on personal computers using spreadsheets. It quickly went from VisiCalc to Lotus 1-2-3 and then to Lotus Symphony with integrated word processing and graphics. It was fun to be an early adopter of such powerful new tools. Software even turbocharged analysis with an ability to make the numbers talk in documents and graphs. The PC accelerated my learning that financial statements can really talk if you can visualize the real-life behavior and drivers reflected in the numbers.

I decided to seek a summer internship in Minneapolis and was hired by Cowles Media Company, owner of the *Minneapolis Star Tribune* newspapers among others. Working in the treasury group for the CFO, I had the opportunity to visit Wall Street and investment banks to review annual reports of other media companies in preparation for the finalization of ours. It was at Cowles that I was introduced (not in person but through his annual letters) to Warren Buffett. He competed with Cowles when Berkshire Hathaway bought the *Buffalo Evening News* in 1977. Cowles had owned the competing newspaper in Buffalo but closed it in 1982 following years of losses in a fight to the death with Buffett. The losses and write-offs left an indelible mark on Cowles's financial statements, and I just had to understand what led to these losses and write-offs. I decided to look at Berkshire's side of this story. Understanding an industry and market by studying the companies playing in it became a habit for me. Knowing your competitors and how they present to the customer you all are trying to win over has immense value.

When the dust settled in Buffalo, New York, Berkshire reported that its *Buffalo Evening News* went from a $4 million loss to a $27 million profit in 1984. They didn't just survive. They won big.

Through this event, Warren indirectly introduced me to market dynamics that had not completely sunk in during business school. As a newspaper grows circulation, its ads and classifieds become more valuable. The newspaper can then invest more in the newsroom and improve the product. This virtuous cycle creates a profit flywheel and increasing returns to scale, which gets tough and expensive to compete with. It was also a real-world lesson in "market signaling" as Buffett made it clear in words and actions that he would never, ever, quit. In fact, he was investing in the newspaper despite substantial losses in a two-newspaper town. Cowles was completely rational when it threw in the towel. The clarity of Buffett's thinking was refreshing. I went on to read all of his annual letters back to the beginning. Here was a guy who played the long game and made sure his competitors and the whole world knew it. I have read every letter since.

My summer internship was incredibly valuable, but it was back to Tuck for my second year, during which I started my search for a real job. With the economy now humming, the market was strong for MBAs, and the interview slots were dominated by investment banks (which advise), consulting firms, and investment companies (which invest). But that seventh-grade paper poked at me again: I wanted to run a business, and I was looking for a pathway to that goal.

One of the culminating experiences of the Tuck program was a one-week computer simulation game called Tycoon. Five students form a company to compete within the global clock industry using a business computer simulation game that cycles through the equivalent of years in the industry. The game is continuously scored on growth and profitability leading to company value, and overall winners are based on who created the most profitable business. The game is set so all the strategic and operational levers are in your control—product strategy, pricing, marketing mix, sourcing strategy, logistics, inventory and receivables strategies, customer focus, and international growth. We were all excited to play this game as it was a chance to use many of the tools that we'd been learning for the last year. In the midst of the game, my second son, Joel, was born, so there was a lot of dashing between campus and the hospital.

My group in the competition formed the Roman Hands company (remember, it's the clock industry, back when clocks still had hands). The game was a blast, but we made an early error of not paying attention to the landed cost of outsourced versus manufactured product. We were growing like crazy, but actually losing money along the way until we discovered the true cost of outsourcing clock production compared to making our own. We quickly recovered and sprinted to the finish line only to get second place, which we celebrated as a victory, given our nearly fatal early errors. There were many lessons, but one was clearly this: Getting it 80 percent right might not cut it. There are many ways to fail in a business, so you must pay attention to everything in the enterprise.

Execution in business, I learned, is akin to moving a wall of bricks forward, a few at a time, but each in sync or the wall will collapse. The wall is your enterprise, and each brick is a set of key priorities. I began to observe that great companies do many things well at the same time. Their success is not an accident. It wasn't as simple as one superstar employee, one winning product, or being the hot brand of the moment. The Tycoon simulation was my first experience with stumbling in execution. Unfortunately, it would not be my last.

My experience at Tuck shaped a lot of the values I would later prioritize at Brooks: Enterprise thinking from an investor and CEO perspective; do the analysis to validate plans; solve for the customer and profitability; have a point of view; develop a competitive strategy you can own; and do it as a team like the groups at Tuck do. It is great if you are smart. But it stops there if you can't bring your teammates along and stand at the finish line together.

The starting pistol fired. I was off and running.

CHAPTER 2

Picking Up the Pace

NOW A FRESHLY MINTED MBA, I was eager to put my education to work and pay off a pile of student debt. Most important, I wanted to get in the game at a real company and continue to learn from what Professor Scott Galloway calls "blue flame thinkers."

I found what I believed would be the perfect opportunity in an analyst role at Pillsbury, the Minnesota food company that had rapidly grown to join the leaders of consumer-packaged goods. Getting the job in corporate development, however, was yet another replay of not making the varsity hockey team until my sophomore year at Hill-Murray and later my deferred admission to Tuck. I had great interviews, but an offer remained elusive.

It was becoming clear that I was not the first choice. The key leaders in the group of candidates included Chicago and Wharton grads, and I knew a Harvard grad who was also interviewing. As the weeks went by with no response, I reached out to a senior leader at Pillsbury, Charles McGill, who was a fellow

Tuck alum and a nationally recognized expert in mergers and acquisitions. He confirmed that offers were going out to several interviewees. But not me. Not yet.

One attribute I carried forward from hockey was persistence. I never gave up digging for the puck in the corners and feeding it to a teammate for the shot. I stuck with the process at Pillsbury, and with a nudge from Charles McGill, I finally got the offer.

Pillsbury hired MBAs into its mergers and acquisitions group with the expectation that after a few years, they would transfer into one of the businesses. That was a perfect scenario for me. From the Pillsbury Doughboy to Häagen-Dazs ice cream and Burger King, this was a haven for building brands. I was excited to be in a challenging role, surrounded by smart and successful people.

I would get the opportunity to work closely with many senior leaders at Pillsbury and learn from them all. One of the most impressive leaders I would ever work with was Jerry Levin. For more than a decade, Jerry had led Pillsbury's corporate development, which became the engine of its growth. He completed dozens of acquisitions with some of the most noteworthy brands of the time, from Green Giant (ho, ho, ho) to Häagen-Dazs, Totino's Pizza, Bennigan's restaurants, and Godfather's Pizza.

→ A Front-Row Seat to Enterprise Leadership

As the marketplace changed and evolved, Pillsbury's growth and earnings were stalling. We were right in the middle of the unfriendly corporate takeover era powered by Drexel Burnham's Michael Milken and his junk bonds. The leadership team at Pillsbury was highly concerned that a corporate raider would soon pounce. In defense mode, Jerry hired several investment banks, including Drexel. The team worked on improving business performance and assessing strategic alternatives to stay independent.

When Bill Spoor, Pillsbury's legendary CEO, was preparing to retire, he chose a replacement who seemed to come straight out of standard casting. He had a statesman's aura: tall, gray hair, immaculate suits, and an eminent presence. But just two years after succeeding Bill, he was struggling. The business was sputtering. I was the analyst working with Jerry as we developed and modeled all the scenarios from divestitures to large transformative acquisitions.

It all came to a head at a momentous board meeting in the Hilton near Chicago's O'Hare International Airport. The new strategy was focused on the spinout of the $700 million Steak and Ale (Bennigan's) restaurant business. I was asked to analyze multiple scenarios that would be presented to the high-powered Pillsbury board in Chicago. Every option was on the table: sell, spin out to shareholders, provide a dividend to shareholders, repurchase shares. Since I had been briefing the executive committee along the way, I was invited to attend the board meeting where, sadly, I watched a CEO essentially face-plant in front of the board. We had worked for weeks to prepare for the meeting, but the CEO had not done the advance work to prepare members of the board for a major strategy shift, and they seemed utterly taken by surprise. The lesson I carried forward was that CEOs must create a credible vision and a long-term plan, and keep the board and the investors behind them. Equally important, CEOs must then execute for competitive advantage in every category.

Pillsbury's new CEO presented before a board comprising fellow CEOs from 3M, Burroughs, and other top brands, as well as the architect and builder of the modern Pillsbury, Bill Spoor. The board and Bill saw his pitch as a repudiation of the restaurant strategy. They were not buying it. With the plan completely rejected, we all boarded private jets for the trip home. It was one of those quiet and uncomfortable rides, kind of like that of the losing team on the bus ride home after being routed in an important game.

Within a few weeks, the board made its decision. The CEO resigned and Bill Spoor came out of retirement to once again serve as the chairman and CEO of Pillsbury. We had a new boss.

Bill, whom the *New York Times* would later herald as the man who turned Pillsbury into a food industry giant, had risen from poverty to become CEO. He had a vision; he was a builder and a driver. Jerry Levin assigned me to serve as a personal assistant to Bill, the best education I could ever ask for.

Bill's main mission was to keep the company together and not sell anything, particularly the restaurant group that included Burger King. Pressure on the company was immense. The *Wall Street Journal* published several front-page articles on the problems at Pillsbury. Bill's tasks included restoring growth, finding a new CEO, fending off activist investors, and rebuilding credibility with the board and with investors.

My work at Pillsbury often felt like it was coming through a fire hose, and it wasn't always about managing a profit-and-loss statement. One afternoon I was asked to present an acquisition analysis on a popular Tex-Mex food chain called Chili's. The entire executive committee gathered in the conference room as I flipped through one overhead projector transparency after another (this was pre-PowerPoint). Early in my career, I got shaky, short of breath, and stammered when I stood to speak. The only antidote was to be so fully prepared that I knew the material better than anyone in the audience. On that day I was ready.

A few transparencies in, I confidently told the CEO and the executive committee that Chili's growth was being driven by a new menu item called *"fuh-jee-tas."* The room erupted in laughter, but I doubled down, "These *fuh-jee-tas* are selling like crazy!"

"Jim, you've got to get out more," the president of the restaurant group bellowed. The menu item, of course, is a *fajita*, but there were not many Mexican food restaurants in the Twin Cities at that time; hence my uninformed Minnesota palate.

Pillsbury would continue to expand my horizons as Bill Spoor took me to dinner on a business trip in Dallas. Being disciplined on my first dinner with the chairman, I decided I would have only one beer. As I'd often heard, make sure you arrive early for a meeting, be better dressed, and drink less than the boss. But of course, as he ordered his second martini, he asked if I'd join him with one. I'd never had a martini. Using good judgment, I replied that I was fine and would pass.

He would not have it and challenged me to try one. "You are fumbling the ball, Jim. Come on, you have got to try one!" He quickly ordered one for me and one for him. Given my dad's past, I vowed never to partake in a boozy meal, but I did enjoy having my first martini with a legend.

→ Pillsbury Had a Few Strong Brands; Many More Struggled

As an advisor to the chairman, I believed the growth and returns puzzle merited exploration. I had written several confidential memos for the executive team on topics including the company's cost of capital and return-on-equity impact of share repurchases. I had also come across a book called *The PIMS (Profit Impact of Marketing Strategy) Principles: Linking Strategy to Performance* by Robert D. Buzzell and Bradley T. Gale. The book's analysis led me to a key insight. A three-dollar can of the iconic Pillsbury Hungry Jack biscuits was nine times more important to a high return on capital than leading market share. The data showed that a low-ticket, consumable, high-frequency product that earns loyalty is more often a high-return business. Pillsbury's crown-jewel brand was the iconic, giggling Pillsbury Doughboy. The brand's three-dollar cans of biscuits or cinnamon rolls had a dominant market share at more than 90 percent in addition to proprietary technology that produced fabulous gross margins and incredible returns on capital. As such, it was a profitable, growing business that allowed Pillsbury to invest in new products and compete for customers.

The Pillsbury Doughboy was also an icon for what Warren Buffett calls a business's moat—an enterprise's ability to maintain a competitive advantage. Unfortunately, that winning formula was not embraced across the company. Pillsbury had been incredibly innovative in areas like microwave technology. It was among the first to develop products for the microwave oven, including popcorn and innovative products like Toaster Strudel. Yet both of these were considered business failures when Pillsbury failed to build defendable, profitable brand positions against the likes of Orville Redenbacher's and Pop-Tarts.

As a young strategy analyst, the moral I took away was clear. If you choose to play, you must play to win. If you are entering a new business with serious competition, you need to prioritize solving for your moat. In business, a moat leverages the medieval castle metaphor, describing a business's competitive advantages that allow it to successfully grow and defend its position with customers profitably against any would-be competitor. Seeing inattention to competitive success was a lesson I would remember when I eventually faced Nike.

Another lesson I learned was about the importance of an empowered culture. Bill Spoor was both loved and feared inside the company, but Jerry Levin seemed to treat him like a peer. He was never tentative in meetings with Bill. When Bill wanted to speed up Pillsbury's acquisition flywheel again and charged our team to develop an aggressive strategy, he gave Jerry specific marching orders. After all, it was in a similar process a few years earlier that Bill had discovered a little ice-cream company in the Bronx with a store called Häagen-Dazs. He spotted its potential, bought it for a few hundred million dollars, and turned it into a blockbuster, billion-dollar brand. Bill told our team he wanted to see recommendations for the next round of acquisitions in a month, so we rallied the troops, diving into databases to create hundreds of acquisition prospects.

A month later, Jerry kicked off the meeting. "Bill, you asked us to prepare a broad-based acquisition screen. We didn't do that. What you should have asked us for was a focused screen against our core strategies and principles, and that is what we will present to you today."

With Bill's reputation for challenging and skewering presenters, Jerry's confidence and willingness to express a point of view with conviction impressed me. It echoed back to Wheelock Whitney at the University of Minnesota and his "good judgment" challenge. In addition, one of my Tuck professors, John Shank, insisted you took a point of view on business issues in the cases we studied. "Pick a side," he advised. "The only things in the middle of the road are dead skunks and yellow lines!" Now Jerry was demonstrating that, no matter your title, you should have a point of view and you should express it, openly. Don't just check the box; think and add value. Earn your salary.

From my vantage point as assistant to the CEO, I was privileged to work with and learn from all of the top Pillsbury executives. I had a great view of opportunities across all of the brands. At my two-year mark, I began searching for a permanent job within one of the business divisions. I considered Burger King and Häagen-Dazs, but ultimately chose to join the Pillsbury Doughboy team. The company's best marketers were in the refrigerated dough business, which included talent from Kellogg's. Consumer packaged goods companies like Pillsbury and Kellogg's were well known for mining insights from consumers and winning their loyalty. They were a breeding ground for talented business leaders. I was assigned to two new product launches: microwave fudge brownies and honey-flavored Hungry Jack biscuits.

There, I learned the art and science of marketing. I attended focus groups, taste tests, package design sessions, and research-and-development meetings to engineer better taste profiles. How do we remove fats but preserve flavors that customers love? I had to select among dozens of photographs of a brownie for the package cover as we tweaked the design for millions of grocery shoppers. Color, texture, moisture, lighting. Discerning and picking the "fudgiest" photo was a new experience. I also learned not to have lunch before a three-hour biscuit tasting. I worked with Leo Burnett Worldwide, an ad agency headquartered in Chicago, creator of the Pillsbury Doughboy, Jolly Green Giant, Tony the Tiger, and many other iconic characters. We seriously debated for hours whether it was within the doughboy's character to play air guitar on top of a stove. In the end, absolutely! Followed by a tummy poke, of course.

Eventually, Pillsbury could not prevent a takeover. By 1988 the British conglomerate Grand Metropolitan made an unfriendly but ultimately successful offer to buy Pillsbury at a 21 percent premium. The company would change dramatically. Most of the top thirty leaders were gone within a year. It was time for me to move on.

→ Into the Great Outdoors with Coleman

The quest to deliver short-term results was met by underinvesting in the moat and the subsequent inability to attract customers in the future. In years to come these truths would inform my strategy to compete with Asics, Nike, and New Balance. I had also learned from some of the best marketers in the world at Pillsbury, a decidedly indoor company. I would soon apply what I learned to the small but growing world of enthusiast, performance outdoor, and sports products.

Private equity was beginning to boom in the 1980s, and it didn't take my boss and mentor, Jerry Levin, long to land on his feet. Ronald Perlman, one of the most successful investors at the time, had won control of the Revlon Company in an epic and unfriendly takeover. More important for me, he had recently acquired the Coleman Company of Wichita, Kansas. If you are a camper, glamper, or outdoorsperson of any kind, you likely know Coleman. The company made its name at the turn of the last century for bringing light to the darkness of outside. Its gas lanterns and later its gas stoves, coolers, sleeping bags, and backpacks were synonymous with the outdoors.

Jerry Levin came on board as chairman and CEO of Coleman. I joined as vice president for corporate development along with Mike Ellwein, a senior lawyer at Pillsbury who had been active on acquisitions. Mike was a brilliant lawyer and a wise mentor. One morning at Pillsbury, I filled my coffee cup and went on my way to my next meeting. Mike stopped me cold: "Hey, hey, hey, wait a minute! Am I your mother?"

I looked at him confused.

"You just took the last cup of coffee. Do you expect me to make the next one for you? If you empty the coffee, you make the next pot!" That actually became a life lesson for me, and to date, I think I've made more pots of coffee at Brooks than anyone.

At $658 million in revenue, Coleman was a smaller, more hands-on company. In the first year, I worked on divesting several businesses, consolidating factories, and assessing new ad agencies. I also learned about the importance of accountability. In early 1990, we were about to close the year-end audit when a problem surfaced. At the last possible moment, we discovered significant accounting irregularities within Coleman Spas, a small division in Phoenix, Arizona. Spas was a business acquired as part of a backyard strategy for the Coleman brand. This business was an outdoor hot tub product designed for backyards. The tub featured temperature controls and water jets, a backyard experience to which we would ultimately add Coleman-branded barbecue grills and patio furniture.

As we reviewed Spas's audit results, it appeared that its leadership had inflated both revenue and profitability. The division was shipping product on trucks, and then invoicing revenue at the end of the year against orders that did not exist. The trucks were driving around Phoenix and then returning the product in early January for revenue credit. What's more, the inventories were purposely and dramatically overstated. The company made portable hot tubs that were acrylic shells in redwood cabinets. The wood was accounted for on a board-foot basis. They had well more than $1 million of valuable, clear, horizontal-grain redwood loaded on dozens of pallets in inventory. Unfortunately, much of this inventory was essentially firewood—short, scrap pieces that were not usable in production. It made you want to laugh and cry. They overstated profits by $1 million based on fictional inventory value that was nothing more than kindling off the production floor.

→ A Turnaround Opportunity

We cleaned up the books, and the president was fired. Despite having never managed an employee directly, I went back to headquarters and begged Jerry to let me run the division. I convinced him I could turn it around. In 1990, at age thirty, I became president of a company, a goal I had first written about in seventh grade. I dove into a competitive analysis of the portable spa industry. I benchmarked all the major players, researching everything about their businesses that was available in the public domain. I also studied competitors' product brochures and outlined each company's brand philosophies based on what each one had written about itself. The goal for a brand is not to emulate the competition but to find unaddressed opportunity in between the strengths that your competitors already own. If you were to map out on a blank whiteboard or sheet of paper where your competitors stand in a crowded field, you want to find "white space" or gaps in which to maneuver. More on that in chapter 10.

The business was a mess on many levels, so while I got the job, success would require both a repositioning of the product in the market and a real turnaround. I'm sure the team at Coleman Spas was skeptical about a young, inexperienced MBA and corporate staff guy. What I did not lack was confidence that the business was fixable; that a diligent and comprehensive approach to assessing the business, organization, product strategy, balance sheet, and key marketing stories was vital to energize our dealers and customers and to stem losses. In the first three months, we had a significant layoff, taking our headcount down from approximately 160 to 120 people. I was inexperienced but clinical in my approach. It was a business necessity.

My first big mistake involved the termination of our head of sales. He was the wrong guy in the wrong place. But it was the first time I ever had to fire someone. I invited him to breakfast, but as soon as I started talking, we set down our forks and never touched the food. It was awful. Since then, I've learned much about how to handle separations from a company. When it happens, it's going to be a day that the affected person will never forget. That means respect and dignity are essential in how the conversation is handled. It doesn't matter if it's a foregone conclusion, amicable, a total shock, or combative. You have to handle it professionally and with empathy if their dignity is to remain intact. There is simply no reason to create animosity over how you treat people.

With the layoff behind me, I began to engage with leadership and imbibe a fire hose of learning about managing people and integrating teams. The division was a turnaround project that badly needed clear business goals with metrics across every department, most of which had no plan. Leaders needed to be accountable, but first we had to define what they were responsible for. The business needed hands-on leadership, and I dove deep into every function. I worked with the accounting team to improve our monthly reporting and get my arms around business performance, expenses, and the balance sheet. We needed to up our game on accounts receivable collection. I brought in a talented human resources leader to improve our people management, and I created monthly staff meetings with our top dozen or so people. We commenced regular business reviews. We hired a new ad agency to bring the Coleman brand alive and articulate our product philosophies and differences. We dramatically improved the quality and functionality of the product to get to table stakes in the category. Next, we improved gross margins significantly by cost engineering the product to be easier to manufacture and ship.

Within a year, we turned multimillion-dollar losses into a healthy profit. We began to grow. The team was now stabilized and motivated. Unfortunately, Jerry Levin informed me that Coleman had decided to sell the company. He offered to finance me if I wanted to buy the company and continue to build it. I had flashbacks to our family's restaurant, Weber's Supper Club, back in North St. Paul. But I saw myself as a CEO/builder, not an owner/manager. I did not want to be "married" to a small business. I wanted to build a bigger brand and business, something with a clear, long-term future.

→ Seattle Opportunity Beckons

One August evening in 1991, I flew to Seattle for a Coleman Group meeting. It began with a wonderful dinner on the patio of a Lake Washington restaurant. Back home in Phoenix, daily temperatures were hitting 115 degrees. Our boys played soccer and T-ball games at 7:00 a.m. to avoid the intense heat. They spent the rest of the day either in the swimming pool or indoors to keep cool. But in the Pacific Northwest, it was blue skies and eighty degrees. Looking out at the spectacular water and the Olympic Mountains on the horizon, I could see our family—now five Webers strong with the birth of our third son, Reid—living there. Having lived in the tundra of Minnesota and the desert of Arizona, the rain forest was looking pretty good.

One of Coleman's holdings was O'Brien International, a leading water-sports brand in the growing action sports segment of sporting goods. Long before tech pioneers were founding companies in their garages, Herb O'Brien founded a compression-molded, fiberglass water ski, wakeboard, and kneeboard company in his parents' basement outside of Seattle. He and his boards were legendary, but so was a side business that would later come to light. He went to prison for smuggling cocaine inside water skis under the bindings. He lost his company, though it tried hard to retain a reputation for exciting products. Despite its lack of profitability, O'Brien International was the global category leader, so Coleman acquired it.

By 1992, O'Brien needed new leadership. I leaped at the opportunity to become its fourth president in two years. Mary-Ellen, our three boys, and I relocated to beautiful, ever-rainy Seattle.

Now in the land of Boeing and Microsoft, as well as great outdoor brands like K2, Eddie Bauer, and REI, I was surrounded by entrepreneurial inspiration. I also faced another turnaround. O'Brien had significant losses, weak margins, tired products, declining market share, and an urgent need for action.

Perfect!

I recruited several key executives and nurtured and motivated a team focused on building strong foundations for the business. Then I led an aggressive six-month effort to totally revamp the product line, marketing communications, promotional support, sales programs, and the sales force. We addressed customer needs and won trade acceptance while improving gross margins. We fully implemented a new computer system in eight months to integrate all functions and reduce administrative costs. We also implemented sweeping changes in the way we did business, such as developing a plan to consolidate factories and warehouses to reduce overhead and significantly improve customer service. We restructured the European distribution network to gain focus and improve margins.

Within two years, we had repositioned the product line and the sales program. Market share, profits, and gross margins were now growing.

→ Managing a Brand Is Fun; Growing a Brand Is Hard

My boss, George Napier, gave me positive feedback that I had successfully turned around two companies. He continued by saying that, while that was admirable, I hadn't yet proved that I could grow a brand. It stopped me cold, because I knew he was right. Pillsbury, Coleman, and O'Brien had not yet taught me how to grow a brand organically and add new customers to it.

In 1996, I was approached by a group of investors to lead Sims Sports. It was an opportunity to run an independent company and grow a brand in the white-hot snowboard category. I took the challenge. After ten years, I would be off the mothership on which I had set sail with Jerry Levin at Pillsbury and then Coleman. It would be a choppy ride.

Much like Herb O'Brien had created modern water skis and wakeboards, Tom Sims had pioneered snowboarding, becoming world champion in 1983. The company's board of directors, comprising both founders and new investors, was incredibly divided. From the very first board meeting, the new investors felt they had overpaid and been misled on the deal. I struggled to get them all to focus and come together to support the business.

With a shakeout coming in the industry, I had been hired to consolidate Sims's three entrepreneurial organizations into one global team, and focus on revitalizing product innovation, growing sales, and building the brand. I dug in and did what I do best: looked for unaddressed opportunities to bring value to the snowboarder. With literally hundreds of brands making boards, we decided to develop a binding with tooling costs high enough to create real barriers to entry. The team created the "Link" binding, which had several innovations and patents as well. We improved the product development process, focusing on enthusiasts who demanded technical superiority at all price points. We won design awards and began once again to compete with industry leaders on performance and quality. We saw two consecutive years of sales and margin growth with Market Strength Index ratings (as measured by a respected, independent, syndicated dealer survey) rising from fifteenth to fifth in two years. Overall improvement was first or second in every survey category.

But dysfunction persisted on the board. I still could not get them unified and focused on the plan. We were like oil and water. By 1998, they were through with me, and I was through with them. Today, I refer to this job as my career mulligan. But the lessons learned would prepare me to proactively solve for my investors' goals in the future.

Another huge silver lining of my time at Sims was a relationship I struck with J.H. Whitney & Company, a private equity firm I had pitched when we needed investment funds. Whitney had recently acquired Brooks Running, a nearly hundred-year-old brand that competed with Nike a few hours south in

Beaverton, Oregon. Whitney needed someone it knew in the Pacific Northwest who could sit on the board as an independent representative. I already knew the Brooks CEO, Helen Rockey, and so I accepted the board role. I also returned to banking, joining Piper Jaffray's Seattle office to open a middle market mergers and acquisitions practice.

It was a rewarding time. I was creating broad connections in the consumer products world, and my board work at Brooks and Nautilus, Inc., kept me close to a few interesting brands. However, things were getting serious at Brooks. The company had undergone multiple ownership and leadership changes. As conversations on the board shifted from growth to survival, the partners at Whitney, led by Paul Vigano, rolled up their sleeves and dove in to understand what was happening.

The chairman of Brooks's board, Ann Iverson, looked down the table at me during a particularly stressful board meeting. "Jim," she said, "you should be in here running this business."

Brooks was super tempting. I loved leading a company. I loved the product. I loved running. For me, life was family, work, and a hobby, and my hobby was running. Over the next ninety days I engaged in many private conversations with Brooks board members and Whitney partners to find a path for Brooks to survive and for Whitney to salvage its investment. Whitney's president, Peter Castleman, would opine: "Look, this is a mess. We didn't really understand what we bought. This company is trying to be everything to everybody. It might take you five years, but you've got to pick a path and make it stand for something."

→ Forming a Personal Leadership Manifesto

I had learned marketing at one of the world's great consumer packaged goods (CPG) companies, Pillsbury, and turned around several brands in the outdoor space. I had now spent nearly ten years running three different companies. I took some time to think about Whitney's pitch. With nearly twenty years of management experience under my belt, what had I learned that might help Brooks succeed? I reread old business plans, spoke with my wife, talked with colleagues, and churned through my life's lessons during my runs. I knew what a great business driven by a brand with a moat looked like. And more important, I now knew how to build one. Reading about Warren Buffett's love of brands—their ability to capture market share and drive repurchase by loyal customers—had a great influence on

A Value Creation Flywheel:
Premium Brand + Disciplined Business Model

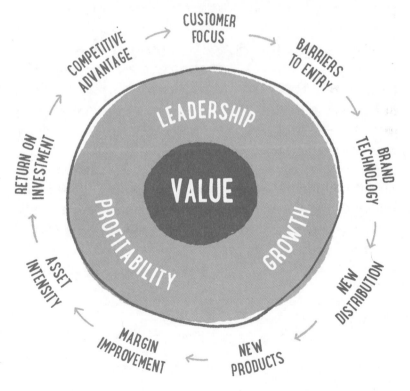

Figure 1

me. I had used the chart in figure 1 to explain the return on investment (ROI) flywheel that great businesses nearly always had: a unique brand position with high margin products and the potential for repeat customers.

I landed on four leadership principles that I knew were essential for long-term success and would begin to form my leadership manifesto:

1. **Own a Niche:** Pursue greatness by simultaneously owning a niche, growing, and delivering premium profits consistently and over time.

2. **Build a Moat:** Create a distinctive, defendable brand proposition. Getting credit for it from the customer (at full price) is the measure of its strength and essential to sustainable success.

3. **Solve for Profitability:** Engineer it into your business model. If successful, it can create a flywheel of investment to strengthen your moat.

4. **Vision without Execution Is Hallucination:** Dreams and plans are meaningless if they're not backed by action. Walk the talk.

In the spring of 2001, I called Paul Vigano at Whitney and agreed to take the helm at Brooks Running. It was the second time I'd become a company's fourth president in two years.

CHAPTER 3

Pivot #1: Running Only

THE SECRET TO SUCCESS IS CONSTANCY OF PURPOSE. On my first day at Brooks, I wrote this Benjamin Disraeli–attributed quote on my office whiteboard. It has remained there. The point was to obligate me to focus, to play the long game, and to not get distracted.

I had no intellectual connection to Disraeli, but his statement captures my conviction that sustained focus coupled with purpose is essential to success. Brooks lacked both when I joined, and I aimed to remedy that. So, in my early days as CEO, I regularly warned team members that they would grow tired of hearing me repeat the mantra that Brooks is a performance running brand, period. We were not going to chase bright shiny objects. We would hear many pitches for investing in this or that and get regular advice to expand our lines into this or that category from kids' shoes to basketball. In the 1980s, rollerblading exploded in popularity, but it crested and crashed. Hockey players like me get rollerblading, but is it endemic to humans? No, not really. Running is and always has been. Running is at the center of every sport, and we would not take our eyes off it. We needed to solve for the customer—first, last, and always.

One April morning in 2001, I drove downtown through Seattle's cloudy spring weather for the annual gathering of Brooks's international distributors. I was two weeks into my role as CEO and was facing a room full of our global partners for the first time. It was gray and raining outside, darker in the hotel lobby, and the mood inside the conference room was downright gloomy. The company had lost $5 million and had more than $30 million in debt. We had massive inventory issues, including millions of dollars in apparel fabric that was obsolete. Brooks hadn't hit its numbers for years, and those banks funding the company wanted out. The dot-com bubble had burst, and the world was in the midst of a serious economic downturn. The attacks of 9/11 were still five months away. Our distributors who were not mad were worried. Brooks was in trouble, and the entire industry knew it.

To make matters worse, the competitive marketplace in performance athletic footwear above $100 was all about visible technology. Nike was riding high with its tried-and-true Air line of shoes, and Shox had just been introduced with much fanfare. Asics had its popular Gel line, and retailers like Big 5 Sporting Goods and Foot Locker enjoyed reminding us that Asics had a dozen or more technologies in their shoes, which helped clerks on the retail floors sell them. In every price segment and retail channel, Brooks was in sixth or seventh place in sales. Nike, Adidas, Reebok, New Balance, Asics, and Saucony were all ahead of us.

I knew what I was in for, mostly. When I stepped into that dark conference room, my mood was surprisingly confident, perhaps annoyingly so. As a Brooks board member, I had studied the market carefully. We had a plan to survive in performance running gear, even if it would prove controversial at first. I knew the market was there. Road race participation, that growing community of joggers and runners of every capability, had increased 25 percent over the previous five years. On a graph, the trajectory for running looked like an amazing investment. A big factor was women's participation.

Title IX, enacted at the apex of the previous running boom in 1972, had created a new generation of runners. A new health and wellness boom was underway, with running at its core. In 1967, Kathrine Switzer was repeatedly assaulted by the Boston Marathon's race director in an attempt to stop her from running. It wasn't until 1972 that women were openly and officially allowed to register for the Boston Marathon. Nearly thirty years later, running was once again exploding, but very few shoe brands (including Brooks) appeared to notice. Instead, we were all competing for sales to the masses, trying to cover every sport and every price point with visible technology that had eye appeal on the shelf. Performance running was a backwater. Nike and Adidas were winning overall but losing market share within the category. New Balance and Asics were doing better within the higher-priced running market.

Running was, and still is, the biggest category in athletic footwear and apparel. I felt then that if we focused and got a small piece of it, we could not only survive but build a meaningful brand and a valuable business.

That morning, as I clicked through a few slides on the state of the company, I sensed eyes rolling. Fair enough. I was just another in the long line of Brooks CEOs—the fourth in the past two years alone. But at least they were hearing facts and the truth about our predicament. Overall, sales were well short of plan, shipments were late, projections were too aggressive, and distribution channels were not in sync.

I had already heard that there was an employee pool going for how long I'd last. But, on slide eight, the room hushed, and our audience began to sit up in their seats.

"What will Brooks be?" I asked.

Breaking the tape in 2:09:00, Brooks athlete Greg Meyer wins the 1983
Boston Marathon, an American title he held until 2014. The year before
his Boston victory, Meyer placed first in the Chicago Marathon. It would
take another 35 years for an American to win that race.
Courtesy of PCN Photography/Alamy Stock Photo

Going forward, I told them, we would pivot to a running-only
brand. Real performance for real runners. Our product would
perform for the most discerning runners, earning their trust
mile after mile, and our brand would embody the spirit and
soul of all who run. We would be serious about the running
lifestyle and celebrate the positive energy gained from it. We
would satiate the endorphin addict. Our product line would be

the best running shoes, the best running bras, running socks, and running apparel. Running, running, running.

Our customer focus would be active runners, period. From competitive racers to weekly fitness runners. Brooks would build engineered performance gear and price it accordingly. Our gear would serve the sport and the enthusiast lifestyle, not casual use, not family footwear, and not fashion. The room grew quieter still.

→ Moving a Wall of Bricks Forward

Founded in 1914 by a student at the University of Pennsylvania (home of the Penn Relays), Brooks had tried in its earlier decades to be all things to all athletes—runners, wrestlers, skaters, and football, basketball, and baseball players. From the beginning, Brooks had used the standard athletic footwear playbook. The consensus was that you needed at least three legs of a stool: running, court, training, and so on. In addition, you needed to play the game of "good, better, best" pricing strategies across retail channels from a $100-plus performance product to accessible athletic styles (now referred to as "athleisure") priced at $60 to $80, to sporty family footwear priced at $30 to $50. The secret for many of the big brands was that half of their athletic shoes would never go for a run, play basketball, or work out in the gym. In 2000, more than 50 percent of Brooks's sales were in the $30 sporty family footwear. At Brooks we called them "barbecue" shoes because that's what they were actually used for; that, and mowing the lawn. Today they would be categorized as athleisure footwear.

In 1999, J.H. Whitney & Company, the private equity firm that acquired Brooks the year before, asked me to serve on the Brooks board. Shortly after Whitney's purchase, Brooks's CEO Helen Rockey left the company after seven years at the helm. She had successfully turned the company around, pointed the brand to running as its North Star, and turned multiyear losses to a profit. Under two successive presidents after Helen, the business began to drift. Losses returned. Now, since the company had taken on millions of dollars in debt as part of the sale to Whitney, the margin for error was razor thin.

By the fall of 2000, Brooks was in crisis. We were having weekly board calls because the bank was refusing to fund operations. There was a question whether payroll checks would bounce. As plans were being missed, the banks were demanding more capital be put into the business, so Whitney and the board were actively trying to assess how bad things were with customers, suppliers, management, product, inventories, and cash flow.

After the board asked me to run Brooks, we spent three months digging into the numbers, trying to find a path to stem the losses and a strategy that Brooks could succeed with profitably. In March 2001, I spent a day with several Whitney partners in their Connecticut offices to assess the challenges and close the deal to come into the company. The key was Whitney's support. At Brooks's darkest hour, with no guarantees of success, Whitney agreed to recapitalize the company with $7 million to put it on a solid footing. That was all I needed. On April 4, 2001, I was named Brooks's CEO.

The vision to rebuild was becoming clearer, but I had some serious obstacles to overcome. When I told the board I had ten critical priorities, board members advised me to pick just four. I recalled the metaphor I had learned in business school: that success requires moving a wall of bricks forward, as there are many ways to fail. I told the board: "Actually, we do have to do all of these things or we're not going to get there. We're not going to make it."

One of the first challenges was to convince my new team that we could in fact walk (or run!) and chew gum at the same time. We could drive leadership, growth, and profit without skipping a beat. Many employees thought I was just there to sell the company and walk away. I acknowledged that the current owners would need to sell Brooks. The banks wanted out, and they would need a return. But I was convinced that this brand could succeed with a singular focus on performance running, and that we could attract investors. With conviction, I told my team that companies with issues get sold while companies with opportunity attract investors. If we could articulate the opportunities for Brooks, there would be so many investors lining up to back the company that we'd have to hire a parking lot attendant!

Our shoe box is a particular shade of blue. We call it Brooks Blue, or PMS300 in the Pantone Matching System. I wanted to know what it would take to see more and more Brooks Blue boxes coming out of the back room. I knew we had a good chance of getting the sale if we could get customers to try on our shoes. In fact, research confirmed that if we got a shoe on a customer's foot, we won the sale more than 60 percent of the time.

Not long after that presentation in the downtown hotel conference room, I hit the road to meet with customers.

→ Brooks's Runner Focus Leads to Distribution Choices

Throughout that first spring and summer, I met with dozens of our retail partners to test ideas and listen to feedback. One visit was with Big 5 Sporting Goods. In the previous year, it was by far Brooks's biggest customer with $10 million in gear sales out of $60 million in total revenues. Our sales team was nervous I would screw it up. I walked into the meeting knowing that our average shoe price at the big sporting goods stores was about $30, and at that price we were losing money. The margins were so narrow that at best we were just trading dollars. We were carrying millions of dollars in inventory, all financed by our bank.

During the meeting, one of the leaders at Big 5 Sporting Goods looked at me and said, "Jim, we love Brooks. We see a lot of opportunity with Brooks, but we really see your shoes at a $19.99 price point. That's where the opportunity for Brooks is." I thought to myself, *okay, this is over.* There was no way we could be profitable at that price. I went back to Seattle, and we didn't lift a finger on that book of business. We just let it trail out to zero because there was no win there for us or our customer.

A *Runner's World* survey at the time found that price and appearance were among the least important shoe attributes to runners. Fit and comfort ranked first followed by injury prevention and performance features. We cut 60 percent of our product line, and revenues fell as I knew they would. Pivots like this can be lonely. Dropping big national accounts looked like a huge risk. But it had to be done. I knew it would eventually reduce losses and inventory, generating badly needed cash.

Our plan was to prioritize time and resources on partnerships with running specialty stores that sold performance products to runners. In your hometown, think about those stores that cater exclusively to runners. In Seattle, for example, one is Super Jock 'n Jill. Drive past its flagship store on Green Lake and you will see runners jogging up and down the sidewalks trying out new shoes. The store was originally opened in November 1975 by Laurel James, a single mother of five boys. One of Laurel's sons, Chet James, began managing the store in 1981 and later purchased the business with his wife, Judy Albrecht, in 1997. Super Jock 'n Jill is regarded as a trusted resource in the Pacific Northwest for running and walking shoes, athletic apparel, and top-notch customer service.

Stores like Super Jock 'n Jill are curators of the very best running gear. They are the gatekeepers, the epicenters of running in their communities. Knowing we had to earn their trust in both our products and our reliability to service demand, we began to treat them like kingmakers.

Fleet Feet is another important curator of the best running gear. In 2001, its CEO and owner was Tom Raynor, a Brooks alum who had grown Fleet Feet from a single store to more than ninety stores in thirty-four states and the District of Columbia. I was invited to the Fleet Feet Conference in a mountain resort not far from its headquarters in Carrboro, North Carolina.

Tom and I met for lunch outside on a patio. He had watched all the turnover in Brooks leadership and had been briefed on our running-only strategy. With genuine concern, he told me he was worried: "We care about Brooks, and we need you to succeed. We're just not sure you can survive in run only."

Every industry develops conventional wisdom, and there is peril in falling in line with it. Often it seems to reflect the market leader's path to success or the short-term, low-hanging fruit that can be captured in sales. Conventional wisdom leads to merchandising to the obvious, versus creating unique or compelling solutions. In footwear, many believe the conventional wisdom that says brands must play in all categories, across myriad price points. They believe that a company can't survive by playing a narrow game. Our contrarian philosophy was to focus only on premium running, turning a narrow focus into a strength. Remember that we had previously walked away from non-premium running to concentrate on performance running, eliminating 50 percent of our product line and 40 percent of our retail partnerships.

Our remaining partners worried about Brooks's departure from conventional wisdom, which originated when shoe brands owned their own factories. Back then, they needed to play across categories and price points, spreading risk over many sports, categories, and seasons to keep their factories and employees busy. If you choose just running, how do you survive the fashion cycles as running declines or basketball rises? To address the market, you need all price points from $30 through $150 or more per pair. No major brand had ever just focused on one segment. Our bold announcement about premium running did not sound smart to the industry.

While it's no longer necessary to manufacture a full array of sports shoes year-round, companies must have precise quality control. Large brands learned this the hard way when they failed to focus across their entire supply chain on consistent fit critical to runners. Early in our run strategy focus, retailers told us the popular Nike Pegasus running shoe fit differently depending on which of its many factories produced it. We'd seen that movie before. Runners become loyal to specific shoe styles. If you mess up the fit, you risk losing them forever. Brooks made the decision to invest heavily in wear testing. We now have a community of a hundred thousand runners who give us real-time feedback on every shoe across multiple sizes before we hit commercialization. We get a ton of feedback, some good and some bad. But it's always constructive.

"My foot felt like it was sailing!"

"I never had to break them in. I put them on, and I can run miles in them. This is how you know when the shoes fit great."

A specialty store retailer told us that we have the "ahh" factor. People put on the shoe, stand up from the stool, and just say, "Ahh."

And when a shoe doesn't seem quite right, we listen: "I need more stability." "The shoe wasn't flexible enough." "More room in the toebox."

→ Specialty Run Stores: You Are Who Sells You

It was clear to me that our specialty run retail partners really cared about Brooks running shoes and wanted to see our plan succeed. On another visit, I met with the head merchant at Road Runner Sports, at the time the biggest buyer of running shoes in the world.

"All right, Jim, welcome aboard, fourth CEO in two years, good luck, heard it before . . . but we're rooting for you. Just, whatever you do, don't screw up that culture, because when you walk through the doors at Brooks, it's glass-half-full. The people are positive, and they're trying to solve problems, make things happen, and they look like they are having fun."

The Brooks culture had been deeply rooted in running, and now it would be exclusively focused on high margin performance running gear at premium prices. If the products worked, we had a shot at winning the trust of the frequent runner who bought an average of 2.6 pairs per year according to *Runner's World*. We focused all of our marketing efforts on where runners ran and where they shopped. We worked to earn the trust of key influencers starting with specialty run shop owners, managers, and staff.

By 2002, our distribution strategy shifted completely to focus not on being where shoes were sold but where runners shopped for performance gear. This meant we flipped the entire sales strategy to match our product and consumer focus. The company had been focused where the volume was sold and its distribution pyramid had malls (Finish Line and Foot Locker), family footwear (Famous Footwear), sporting goods (Dick's and Big 5 Sporting Goods), and department store chains (Dillard's, Nordstrom, Macy's) as the foundation, plus a narrow block of specialty run shops on top. I flipped the pyramid to prioritize specialty run, then sporting goods and select mall and department store retailers who were focused on runners buying premium performance product (see figure 2). This meant we would be in less than 20 percent of all available doors of distribution for athletic footwear, but the four thousand stores we would focus on were where premium-price running product was purchased.

Our pivot to specialty running was an essential part of our new momentum, but we still had a lot of work to do. Guided by my principle that vision without execution is hallucination, we rolled up our sleeves. We began to build a playbook around a

Figure 2

simple frame, a one-page strategy to get everyone focused. It became a one-page strategy that quickly helped us decide what *not* to focus on.

I worked with our senior leadership team that May to reforecast our business against reality. We lowered our revenue and profit projections so that we could have a fair chance of hitting our numbers and begin to establish credibility. I went to the board with a growing list of to-dos, including cleaning up the balance sheet, liquidating inventory, and reenergizing product development. We reorganized, and I brought in a new and experienced CFO, David Bohan. I shared that one-page strategy and told everyone they would get sick of me repeating it.

The plan required us to gain control of our inventories to improve cash flow and margins by developing and delivering products on time. I had learned from the extreme seasonality of both the summer water-sports business at O'Brien and the snow-sports business at Sims that being on time is not a "nice to have." If you are late, you miss the season. Then you will have inventory left over that you will have to discount to move. To meet demand profitably, it is essential to ship to retailers on time and complete. And it is critical that Brooks not miss full price sales and end up with excess inventories, which kill margins and the value perception of your products. We had to get our product development calendars back on schedule.

→ Performance Brands Are Built on Great Product

In 2001, the Beast and the Addiction were Brooks's most successful shoes, accounting for about half of the company's performance running shoe business, roughly $15 million in revenue. The Beast and the Addiction were number one and number two, respectively, in the industry's motion control category. Beyond those two shoes, Brooks had little else. We needed to strengthen our position in the most important performance segment: the stability category, geared toward runners who need some support but want a lighter, more cushioned, and flexible ride than they'd get with motion-control shoes.

A critical result of our team's refocus on high performance running was the reinvention of Brooks's mid-priced stability shoe, the Adrenaline GTS (Go To Support). The shoe was on its third iteration, and although it hadn't yet caught fire, we knew it had potential if we could nail the product design and then ensure availability. We built it in a one color combo (blue/white) and kept it the same for eighteen months. This allowed us to invest in inventory with little risk and service the demand not to miss a sale. We created a new last, the form over which a shoe is shaped. This tuned the fit, perfected the toe box, and created a well-balanced ride. An even bigger breakthrough was a progressive diagonal rollbar, which used triple-density midsole foam contoured to guide the foot's excessive pronation from the outside in and allow it to transition smoothly from heel strike to toe-off. That fourth version perfected fit, feel, and ride for the shoe.

The Adrenaline GTS 4 also would go on to win *Runner's World's* critical "Best Update" award and Running Network's Gold Medal for "Best Renovation." Today, two decades later, it is recognized as the top-selling stability shoe in the market and one of the best-selling running shoes of all time with more than 30 million pairs sold. One of our shoe testers, who dubbed it the "self-driving car of running shoes," wrote, "This shoe seems to steer your running and protect you from veering off into a lazy or off-kilter stride."

The Adrenaline GTS became *the* franchise product that would save the company and fund investment in growth for the next decade. With our cheap, low margin product out of the way, we could concentrate on the leadership manifesto principles I outlined in the previous chapter: challenging ourselves to lead with runners, grow profitably, build a moat around our brand, and execute with urgency.

As the Adrenaline GTS took off, Brooks began to make headway in other categories. The Glycerin and the Ghost gave us some traction in the market for neutral shoes, generally recommended for runners who don't need support. We launched our first real technical trail shoe, the Cascadia, just as Brooks athlete Scott Jurek began to dominate on the ultra-running circuit.

→ Growing the Brand a Pair of Feet at a Time

We were making progress. But runners are a discerning crowd. You have to earn their trust. Martin Rudow, the editor and publisher of *Northwest Runner* (published from 1976 to 2016), came to visit our offices, then in Bothell, a suburb north of Seattle, to ensure we were carrying the torch. In his essay, Martin ran a photo of me, the new president and CEO of Brooks, climbing a hill in a local half-marathon. He also wrote from his heart: "Healthy shoe companies sponsor races and special events, and help out individual athletes. In short, a healthy shoe industry benefits all of us, and a healthy nearby shoe company should benefit us the most. That's why Brooks is so important to us."

I believed we could survive, but our journey was not for the faint of heart. We had jettisoned every shoe under $75 and would no longer make or sell them. Even so, we made our numbers that year and the team earned its first bonus in a long time. Little by little, things improved. In the first nine months, we generated a lot of cash by moving excess, aged inventory and not investing in unprofitable, cheap shoes. We started to feel a little more pep in our stride. The opt-in employee fun run we held from Brooks's headquarters on Friday afternoons picked up its pace. With the new Adrenaline, we were increasing market share, and in meetings we enjoyed a little trash talk about competitors. The billboard at the Atlanta Olympics from the leading brand proclaimed, "You don't win silver, you lose gold," which left a lot of people out. "Just Do It" may motivate some, but we were out to earn the trust of millions of runners by doing one thing and doing it well: building the best running gear in the world.

Brooks was moving up in the pack, so much so that our internal shorthand for momentum became, "On your left," the universal running signal for passing another runner from behind. It was time to raise our voice through smart marketing. Everything we did supported our more ambitious goals: performance running leadership, focused quality growth, and industry-leading profitability. To get there, we put all of our resources behind product leadership, great customer service, and getting runners and key influencers excited about our products and the brand.

Of course, Nike spent more on marketing by 10:00 a.m. each day than we could spend all year. But we committed to authentic, passionate, energetic marketing that would create a real community for runners—from the grassroots to online and events. The business goal was to drive trial for our new products, but we also wanted to stand out as the brand committed to celebrating your run. Brooks's vice president of marketing, Dave Larson, led the creative efforts to develop entertaining, runner-centric campaigns. In the years to come, we offered a VIP porta-potty experience for runners wearing our shoes. We also offered a booth at the Chicago Marathon that provided a photo op with a giant pasta bowl and a massive meatball. We made an ad featuring one of our elite athletes struggling with our motto, Run Happy. "Yeah," she deadpanned, "we all want to kick ass, but we should have fun doing it." Our ads spotlighted real runners, not models.

The president of Running Network, Larry Eder, told a journalist that Brooks's entertaining campaigns highlighted the excitement of running. "With limited marketing dollars, they get way more value than bigger companies." That was true, in part because we were so targeted. Every marketing effort and all of our people were focused on runners, and we didn't mind if non-runners had never heard about us.

→ Success Attracts Investors

In 2004, Brooks's story, products, distribution, and results confirmed the prediction I had made to our team from the beginning: Investors would come calling. Several years after the pivot to performance running, Brooks was attracting new attention among investors, not to mention media and retail. Sales growth, profit margins, and returns on capital were in the top quarter of the industry. We had a backlog of orders, and revenues were up 26 percent from the previous year. Nike had signed LeBron James and Kobe Bryant. The swoosh acquired Converse, and Phil Knight stepped down as CEO and president.

Another century-old brand, Russell Athletic, took notice. Russell has been the brand on uniforms ranging from the Eagles to the Cowboys, Rams, and Ravens, as well as Auburn University football and every team in Major League Baseball.

In 2004, Russell, which had acquired Spalding among others, bought Brooks for $115 million (nine times our EBITA— earnings before interest, taxes, and amortization), and we were excited to have a new investor who understood sports. Russell CEO Jack Ward told reporters the acquisition was about our leadership in performance running products.

By the spring of 2006, five years after I'd become CEO at Brooks, Warren Buffett's Berkshire Hathaway acquired Russell, driving up its stock by 35 percent. Russell, Brooks, and the other sports brands under Russell joined Berkshire Hathaway's Fruit of the Loom subsidiary, which Warren had purchased out of bankruptcy a few years earlier.

Our owners at Russell saw that Brooks had a plan and it was working. But it wasn't always a given that we would earn and keep their support. I felt that I had to constantly sell our plans and twist arms for support to execute our vision. By now it was clear Brooks had earned a ticket to the big game in athletic footwear and apparel. While we were not a great company yet, we were taking the high road and beginning to execute consistently on delivering the three key elements: leading our niche, growing, and making premium profits.

It was prophetic that I had gone to school on Warren Buffett's idea of building economic moats—creating competitive advantages that are meaningful to customers. Even if my bosses at Russell and Fruit did not quite understand what we were doing at Brooks, I was confident that over time Warren Buffett and Charlie Munger, his partner and vice chairman at Berkshire Hathaway, would.

Our fit–feel–ride promise would become part of our moat. We knew if we won the trust of runners at mile twenty, they would buy our brand again. The way we deliver product to retailers, on time and consistently, is part of our moat. We don't have classic network effects from a platform, network, or monopoly. But if you can create loyalty with franchise products like the Adrenaline GTS, in turn creating word-of-mouth and attracting repeat buyers, those franchises can gain volume scale advantages, driving both lower production costs and broader distribution to increase sales opportunities. Soon you can invest more in innovation and marketing than the other brands. Couple that with world-class inventory management, and you can realize tremendous momentum.

Paul Carrozza, footwear editor at *Runner's World* and owner of the RunTex chain of specialty run stores in Austin, Texas, at the time, caught on quickly. He told a reporter that we were on the upward swing. He noted that our Beast and Adrenaline GTS were among the top-selling shoes for the first time. John Horan at *Sporting Goods Intelligence* wrote that Brooks was now selling to a more lucrative market and coming out on top. Insiders were seeing the construction of a moat.

CHAPTER 4

Becoming an Authentic Leader

BUILDING AN AUTHENTIC BRAND would require consistent, authentic leadership from Brooks and from me. And it wouldn't happen overnight. As a result of our decision to become a premium running brand, casting off the old distractions of low-end product, and chasing multiple sports, Brooks finally had wind at its back. We were catching up. But we were not yet surging ahead. We all knew more was possible. We needed to turbocharge the momentum of that flywheel. Sims and O'Brien taught me how to solve for the short-term wins that bankers, investors, and some board members demand. Private equity will look you in the eye and say it wants to invest over five to seven years. Often, it needs to see results in just three to five years. But by this time in my career, I knew that true success and creating real value required solving for competitive advantage in the longer term, building a distinctive, trusted brand. It takes time to get a team of people to see your vision, believe in its possibilities, and follow you. It takes time to earn customers' trust.

→ For a Brand, Behavior Is Destiny

I believe that a brand is what it sells, where it is sold, and who buys it. In 2001, Brooks's biggest business had been $30 athletically styled family footwear. That needed to end. We could not earn trust with runners while the bulk of our volume was in cheap, casual athleisure shoes. So, we symbolically "burned the boats" by getting rid of everything that was not runnable, including big clunky athletically styled shoes used more for backyard barbecues and mowing the lawn than moving swiftly along roads, trails, and tracks. We eliminated basic foot coverings, refocusing only on performance.

Authentic brands in outdoor and enthusiast sports almost always had their genesis in innovative, breakthrough statement products that elite athletes or enthusiasts fell in love with. Nike had the waffle trainer and the Cortez in the 1970s. Prince delivered an ace for tennis pros and novice players alike when it introduced the Classic racquet with its oversized head and much larger "sweet spot." Callaway did it with the original Big Bertha driver, and everyone in your foursome on the tee saw it happen. North Face built its brand on the iconic Denali jacket. Peloton, with its smart bike and workout experiences. Lululemon, with its premium yoga pants.

We needed to make a statement with product and gain the loyalty of the most discerning customers. We picked the largest category in performance running: the mid-priced stability trainer, where Asics dominated. Our statement product would be the Adrenaline GTS, which would go on to sell four million pairs per year and lead the category. Next, we would add a cushioned shoe alongside the Adrenaline GTS. Eventually our Ghost shoe would also lead its category and sell more than four million pairs per year.

→ Defining a North Star

Brooks would need more than focus and a few great products if it was going to be an authentic brand. We needed an expressed purpose for a brand that had been founded a hundred years earlier and was now refounded in a new century with a new focus and business discipline. A North Star for everything we would do.

When I arrived, there was a mission statement on the wall in the main conference room. It said that Brooks would become a leader in performance running and one of the most admired companies in the world. To me, a mission was like a campaign—useful for setting company goals, but it often had a beginning, a middle, and an end. Thinking further on it, to be an admired company is aspirational, but as measured and recognized by whom? Often the "admired company" lists either overemphasize current financial performance or are derivative of a beauty contest influenced by "best companies to work for" lists. In addition, being admired is external recognition of outcomes; it does not shine a light on how to actually create those "admired" results. We decided that a purpose was preferable to a mission. Purpose is a forever cause that can permeate everything from the business to the brand to the culture. It is a choice, not an outcome. As people came to know Brooks, our purpose would be evident at our core, and we could clearly communicate it to the world as our reason for being—our North Star.

With our new, exclusive focus on building gear for runners and selling it where they shopped, I turned to our team members to brainstorm the articulation of our purpose. We held meetings with groups of twelve employees at a time to engage them in why Brooks existed and what our purpose was. At one such meeting, we gathered in the Chariot conference room at our headquarters in Bothell. We discussed how the leading gear brands in athletic and outdoor were centered on aspirational, epic achievement: breaking the tape, standing on the podium, summitting the mountain. They also featured athletes at the pinnacle of their sport whom everyone else could emulate. I think everyone at Brooks instinctively knew we were different. Brooks was about you and your run. Our point of view was runner to runner, human to human. Every runner, every human. Whether it was your tenth marathon or your first 5K, whether you finished on the podium or at the back of the pack, we were building product for you and cheering you on your run.

We were getting close to defining a North Star. Nike dominated the run category, and its "Just Do It" call to action was understood by every person who ever competed in a sport. Nike and other brands featured epic athletic achievement and aspirational messaging. Break the tape. Take the gold. "Be like Mike." It was easy to look up in awe at these athletes.

We knew there was a Brooks position that was different, but every bit as compelling, universal, and timeless. We thought Brooks's purpose could occupy a more personal, runner-to-runner ethos that was more accessible and motivational. Was it a call to action like "Run Happy" or "Run, World, Run"? Did we have the stature as a brand to suggest a call to action? Was it better to commit ourselves to an internal call to action and earn runners' support over time?

During yet another of these meetings, I was sitting across the table from one of our marketing managers who inserted the word "inspire" into the conversation. The group discussed how runners need inspiration to begin, to persist, to finish, and to accomplish goals. Inspiration is needed every day, every run, every race. To commit as a brand to *inspire* would call on us to engage with customers rationally and emotionally. Being the leading brand or an admired company was simply an outcome; choosing to inspire runners was a commitment we could act on. Further, it challenged us to engage our chosen customers on the power of the run in their lives and elicit a response. So, we had the words, and not long after, we planted our flag on a singular purpose:

to inspire everyone to run and be active.

We rooted our purpose in a truth we all instinctively knew: Running is a limitless source of positive energy that can transform a day, a life, and even the world. Our promise is to create the best running gear, tools, and experiences that move you along your path.

It was a unique position that I believed could define our brand, help us become the best at what we do, and stand the test of time. In every meeting, inside and outside the company, I began to present Brooks's strategic approach on a single page (see figure 3). More than twenty years later, we are still executing this strategy, although we have evolved with the runner, scaled it, and added digital distribution and communication pipes. At a glance, the chart reminds us of Brooks's North Star: Our purpose is to inspire everyone to run and be active. That purpose guides our brand positioning, customer promise, and business model.

If the purpose answers *why*, our competitive strategies answer *how* we will compete and present to the customer, and our strategic goals describe *what* we will accomplish. Through product leadership, we design signature product that is the best in each segment and worth the price, leading to strong margins. We want to be the very best in customer service: achieving leadership in specialty run shops; distributing and fulfilling product on time, even if it means twenty-four-hour turnaround; and attaining tremendous service levels while we manage inventory risk. We bring marketing energy to everything we do, telling compelling stories and gaining the trust and affinity of the most discerning people in running: its key influencers. We

BROOKS STRATEGY ON A PAGE

PURPOSE — To inspire everyone to run and be active			
COMPETITIVE STRATEGY	**STRATEGIC GOALS**		
	Performance Running Leadership	**Focused Quality Growth**	**Industry-Leading Profitability**
PRODUCT LEADERSHIP	It all starts with: • Signature product • Technical edge	Best-in-class products in each segment	Unique, distinctive, proprietary products • High margin • Not promotional
BEST-IN-CLASS CUSTOMER SERVICE	• Specialty channel leadership • Better servicing Greater Sporting Goods, Outdoor	• Longer product cycles • Tighter line, in-stock • On-time, 100% fill rate, 24-hour turnaround	Planning and systems support • Great service levels • Minimal closeouts • Minimal chargebacks • Strong inventory and receivable turns
MARKETING ENERGY	Reach key influencers • Create trial • Specialty running retailers • Sports medicine outreach, athletes, coaches, events, trainers	Create vitality, shouting loudly... • PR, running mags, field marketing • Communicate brand ethos • Runner relevance focus	• Great people • Premium brand • Premium products • Premium distribution

Figure 3

knew if we could win the trust of influencers and frequent runners, they would be a stronger brand halo over the long term than a paid athlete or celebrity endorser.

This one-page strategy was tested quickly.

The Asics 2000 series was the best-selling shoe in the world during these years. We estimated they were selling as many as eight million pairs per year, which was huge. But beginning in 2002, Asics couldn't keep up with demand. Meanwhile, our research and development team had made great progress on the redesign of our Adrenaline GTS, a support shoe that would go on to become a best seller. Pete Humphrey, who runs our research-and-development group, had been working with specialty running accounts to pinpoint what runners were looking for in the Adrenaline. Pete came to Brooks from the parent company of Reebok, Pentland Sports, where he had learned shoe design from Britain's legendary cobblers and had honed his skills as a craftsman working with Premier League soccer players. For the Adrenaline, he led the progressive diagonal rollbar, which dramatically improves a runner's motion path. He and his team conducted intensive analyses of runners' pressure points inside his small but growing lab. From their research, we were able to biomechanically engineer a post at the medial arch that allows for progressive support and creates smoother transitions from the midstance phase to the propulsion phase. The Adrenaline GTS 4 was a breakthrough that would portend many future innovations.

We now had a great product and an opportunity to get it in front of more retailers and runners.

Our strategy called on us to be the best in customer service and to have a 100 percent on-time fill rate. If Asics was sold out, we air-freighted the Adrenaline in every size and width. We were determined to chase demand and not miss an opportunity to gain market share with shoes on feet. Staying true to our purpose, we encouraged and serviced the retailer to bring out our Brooks Blue box. It was working. The Brooks flywheel was gaining momentum.

→ The Core of Successful Leadership Is Authenticity

I've always wanted to be really good at something. Ever since team sports and high school, I have been practicing and improving my craft. From the day I set foot inside Brooks, I've continued to learn who I am as a leader, and who I aspire to be.

During a Brooks leadership offsite, a moderator we'd invited to encourage conversation about effective leadership challenged each of us to take the evening and come back the next morning with a one-pager on what great leadership meant to us individually. It had been a long, productive day. I went home that night and made a valiant effort to articulate my leadership viewpoint, but I went to bed without producing something I felt good about.

The next morning I got up and went out for a run. I often process things better while running—it's always been some of my best thinking and "dot connecting" time. Running the trails and roads near Lake Washington, through neighborhoods, past Douglas firs and western red cedars, I thought a lot about great leadership. I recalled the truly inspiring managers I'd had at Pillsbury and Coleman as well as some of the others I encountered later. I do not consider myself to be a great manager, but I do think of myself as a decent leader. What did that mean, and why was it important to my team at Brooks?

When I got home, I sat down while still cooling off from the run, and it all just poured out on the page, a personal manifesto that reflected what I appreciated in the best and most authentic leaders with whom I had worked. At Brooks, I tried to lead people as I wanted to be led. And so I wrote:

I want to be led:

- I do not want to be managed, manipulated, used, told, or tasked, and I do not want to punch a time clock.

I want to be part of something that I can be proud of, something that my friends, partner, family, and the community are positive about:

- A place with a purpose that is admirable and plays a useful role for people.

- A place that has integrity and will not end up in the news as having failed to obey the standards of society or deliver on its promises.
- A place that is going somewhere, has a future, and is ambitious.
- A place that aspires to add something to the world, its industry, and customers. Innovation is underway, and there is a quest to push the envelope and bring new solutions to the market.
- A place that can stand the test of time and not disappear when the first storm hits. I want to be part of a success.

I want to be communicated with in an open and transparent manner:

- Where are we going? What do we stand for? Why do we work so hard?
- Please respect me as a person and do not assume I will follow just because of your title or because I get a paycheck. I want to work at a place that has more psychic payoff than a paycheck.
- I want to be able to fully trust the people who lead and control the agenda of the organization. Secret agendas and relevant, undisclosed information that affect me or the organization will get me spinning. I will hedge my commitment and effort.
- I want the agenda and tone of the organization to be consistent. If it is not predictable, I will not be able to hook my wagon to it for any period of time.
- I want to be able to trust that I will be treated fairly; that results and impact will carry the day, and rewards and recognition will follow in an equitable manner.

I want to learn:

- I want to be exposed to new things, improve my skills, and expand my knowledge.
- I want to have visibility to the bigger picture to put my work in context.
- I want to know a bit about my bosses' stories to understand where they are coming from and how they think.

I want a challenge to be my best self, fully develop my talents, and do meaningful work:

- I do not want to waste time spinning in circles or doing work that has no value or is discarded.

I expect to work hard, so I want to enjoy my work, the place, and the people I spend time with:

- I want time to have some fun, celebrate wins, and socialize with the people I work with.
- I will give a lot of energy to my work, and I want to get energy back from the people I work with.

I need to feel your support and confidence for my work:

- I need to know you are behind my goals and agenda. It is the only way I can act with confidence and be bold.
- In these fast-changing times, being decisive and acting with a sense of urgency is essential. Please do not be tentative or hedge when I am already out of the gate.

I want to work with people who share the goals and values of the organization:

- I want to be part of a team that is cohesive and shares the organization's core values.
- I want to be part of an open club. I want to be on a team that welcomes diverse talents with different styles, experiences, genders, races, and nationalities.
- Rather than waste energy on self-centered internal conflict around personal styles and agendas, I want to spend it on work that will have a positive impact on the organization and the world.

I want to be led.

Later that morning, back at the offsite, I presented what I'd written in a small breakout group. Afterward I heard mixed reactions. Some really appreciated it. One colleague told me it was weird. Either way, each of the manifesto's points is supported by a lifetime of experiences that drive to promises and commitments. Everything I know has come from observing people who are really good at what they do and then incorporating it into my skill set and approach. And of course, others were symbols of what I did not want to be. Those behaviors and attributes were abandoned.

→ The Essence of Authentic Leadership: Focus, Curiosity, and Trust

In the spring of 2019, I was invited to deliver the commencement speech at my alma mater, the University of Minnesota's Carlson School of Management. It was a great honor. They asked me to share the Brooks story and talk about my authentic leadership journey. That May, I stood in front of several thousand undergrad and graduate students, faculty, and their families and friends. I felt a huge responsibility to deliver takeaway value to these graduates who had just completed their degrees and were about to launch into the next phase of their lives. With a firm belief that strong leadership skills are a currency that will always have value in business and life, I gathered my thoughts. For me, authentic leadership can be distilled to three key aspects: focus, curiosity, and trust.

At Brooks, I knew in my first days that to survive, we had to *focus*, and it was my job as CEO to clear a path for my team to do so. If I couldn't deliver clarity of focus, I risked not being followed. Back then and still today, I work hard to pitch the opportunity around our inspiring purpose and being part of a team that is building a unique and successful business and brand right in the middle of the biggest category in sporting goods and one of the most inclusive sports the world has ever known. Just as important, focus also helps people navigate distractions and decide what not to do. Purpose plus sustained focus wins the game.

For me, *curiosity* is about solving puzzles in a constantly changing world. To avoid being a one-hit wonder, you need to develop a great radar as a leader and then, because nothing ever stays the same, be willing to recalibrate. Be a learner, not a knower. A curious attitude often reflects humility in your understanding of the world around you. Solving for customers' needs takes an intense curiosity. At Brooks, we are creating brand affinity in the minds of customers every day. At Berkshire Hathaway, Vice Chairman Charlie Munger reminds us regularly to avoid the ABCs of business decay: arrogance, bureaucracy, and complacency. Others with capital and brains will always be competing to breach your moat and take your customers away. Staying humble, remaining curious, and avoiding complacency are essential, especially following great success. A final point on staying curious: reevaluating and recalibrating don't mean losing sight of your constancy of purpose.

The third attribute I tied to authentic leadership is *trust*. Business and life are still all about people. Happiness and fulfillment come from your relationships with the people in your life who matter to you. For me it's my wife, my kids and grandkids, my family and close friends, and my teammates at Brooks with whom I share our brand-building journey. However, I did not start out with this wisdom. As I said, early in my career I lacked empathy. I was quite wonky and intensely searching for the right answers. For me, that usually meant scrutinizing the numbers, definitely more IQ than EQ. In hindsight, how I won over MaryEllen is still a mystery to me! Given my insular focus and lack of emotional intelligence (EQ), I can only credit her with having tremendous vision and patience. But through the years I learned that human behavior was behind every number and everything in business. Success requires creating relationships with people, and that means generating trust.

At Brooks we aspire to be a trustable brand. It starts with a promise of a positive product experience, but goes much deeper. We are a purpose-driven brand built around the fact that a run will make your day better. We compete with our culture and values. We think if we can express them consistently in everything we do, over time Brooks will resonate with like-minded people. They will trust us rationally and emotionally. In the past thirty years, I have watched so many of our nation's leaders, institutions, businesses, government offices, and religious organizations suffer from a loss of trust. The stories are all too common. It is a time of increasing transparency and scrutiny. People are looking for someone they can trust.

There will always be unaddressed white-space opportunities for authentic leadership. The leadership manifesto I wrote in the midst of our offsite defined authentic leadership for me personally. The four leadership principles of a CEO that I outlined earlier in this book now required a fifth reflecting these personal traits:

1. **Own a Niche:** Pursue greatness by simultaneously owning a niche, growing, and delivering premium profits, consistently and over time.

2. **Build a Moat:** Create a distinctive, defendable brand proposition. Getting credit for it from the customer (at full price) is the measure of its strength and essential to sustainable success.

3. **Solve for Profitability:** Engineer it into your business model. If successful, it can create a flywheel of investment to strengthen your moat.

4. **Vision without Execution Is Hallucination:** Dreams and plans are meaningless if they're not backed by action. Walk the talk.

5. **Lead Authentically:** Focus, curiosity, and trust are foundational to connecting with people. Treat them with respect, integrity, and humility.

We would get a chance to exercise authentic leadership as the world braced itself for major economic tumult and at the same time contemplated abandoning shoes during a reassessment of running.

CHAPTER 5

Defining Moments: The Great Recession and an Earthquake in Running

I N THE WORLD OF RUNNING, economics, and politics, 2008 was an unforgettable year. The great Ethiopian runner Haile Gebrselassie set the world record for marathons at 2:03:59 in Berlin. It was also an Olympic year with the world's best athletes competing in Beijing, including Brooks marathoner Brian Sell representing the United States.

At Brooks, we were much more like a seven-year-old entrepreneurial upstart than a ninety-year-old company. We'd tripled in size since 2000 (see figure 4), but we entered 2008 without momentum. For the first time in that decade, we lost market share due in part to lack of consistency in the fit of key shoes. While our Adrenaline GTS running shoe was still winning new runners in its category, we were just treading water in others. We stalled. Brands are like sharks: If they don't move,

GLOBAL REVENUE

PIVOT — INVEST TO LEAD

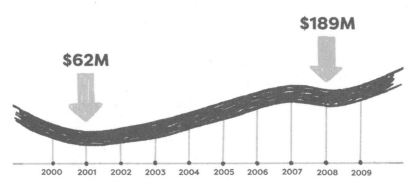

Figure 4

they die. If we are not strong enough in our product offerings and our stories fail to attract new runners, we will lose customers as they choose other brands. Simply put: Every day, brands either get stronger or weaker. Our margins were also under pressure due to increased costs in China driven by higher oil prices, currency fluctuations, and labor markets.

→ The Great Recession Headwind

As summer turned to fall that year, the financial system in the United States was teetering on collapse. You could feel the tension. As a former banker, it was riveting for me to watch. The economy felt like an engine that was over-revving past its redline; clearly something was going to break. As the crisis unfolded, I was taking it all in every morning on business news shows like CNBC's *Squawk Box* and *Squawk on the Street*.

Wall Street fed an explosion of debt to people using their home equity as an ATM machine and buying houses and condominiums with little money down and suspect income verification. These subprime mortgages were then put into pools as mortgage-backed securities, labeled with a AAA rating, and sold around the world. Warren Buffett would refer to the derivative guarantees on these mortgage pools "collateral debt obligations" (CDOs) as "financial weapons of mass destruction." A major bubble was being created with household debt at record levels. Meanwhile, many financial institutions went bankrupt, got put up for sale, or stumbled on as financial zombies. These included Lehman Brothers, Freddie Mac, AIG, Merrill Lynch, Washington Mutual, and Countrywide. It was an uncertain time across the US economy. Money markets froze, affecting companies' ability to finance themselves in overnight markets. At the same time, many individuals' savings were about to freeze or lose value in mutual fund money market programs outside of FDIC protection. The Federal Reserve sprang into action to insure these savings accounts and backstop overnight lending to support the banking system. The term "too big to fail" was born with the Federal Reserve's intervention and Congress's passage of the Troubled Asset Relief Program (TARP), federal legislation authorizing the purchase of massive amounts of mortgage-backed securities and debt.

The coming recession would decimate consumer spending. People hunkered down and wondered if they should bury money in the backyard (that is, if they could stay in their homes long enough to dig a hole).

For Brooks, the effects of a recession were compounded by the effects of an unexpected earthquake in running.

→ The Barefoot Running Earthquake

On May 5, 2009, journalist and author Christopher McDougall published *Born to Run: A Hidden Tribe, Superathletes and the Greatest Race the World Has Never Seen*. The book was, for many, an inspiring story about the freedom of running on trails in the mountains. It ignited a trail- and ultra-running boom led by Scott Jurek, one of the most accomplished ultra-runners of the decade. Jurek was both an important character in *Born to Run* and a Brooks-sponsored athlete who helped us design the Cascadia, a best-selling, trail-running shoe. McDougall's book, however, told the story of human evolution, describing how we once ran down wild game over long distances to survive, and that we did so barefooted and without injury, purportedly. In more than three hundred pages, the author wrote about the Tarahumara, the indigenous people in the Copper Canyons of Mexico, who run as a cultural practice and at elite levels shod in minimalist sandals. Inspired by his running partner, Barefoot Ted, McDougall makes a case that we were actually "born to run" without modern running shoe technologies and that the evils of consumer marketing have fooled us all into believing that cushioning, stability, arch support, and other running shoe features were essential. Worse yet, McDougall writes, running shoes created problems. Lured by the book's claims and the primal running experience depicted in its pages, runners rushed with curiosity to try barefoot and minimalist shoes, driving sales to 20 percent of the performance run category. The Vibram "five fingers" shoe began to appear on the roads, at races, and on celebrity feet on red carpets and fashion runways.

It was a wake-up call for the entire performance running shoe industry. For nearly forty years, Brooks had built highly cushioned shoes as well as stability shoes for runners who thought they needed them. Our biggest franchise shoes at the time included highly engineered, cushioned foams and biomechanically designed, higher-density, diagonal rollbars for people seeking stability. Now the "Born to Run" debate was raging. Advocates claimed that running barefoot, or at least in minimalist shoes, was the holy grail. A number of brands sprinted like jackrabbits (or perhaps lemmings) toward the barefoot movement. In fact, given the industry cost pressures, many runners rightfully suspected that the minimalist shoe movement was really all about cutting the cost of building a shoe.

It was an unsettling time for a performance product company. Could shoes actually be causing injuries? The customer was suddenly wondering whether running shoes could be a bad thing, let alone whether the right shoe could enhance their run, comfort, and maybe even prevent injury. We had to dive into these questions, find answers, and get into the conversation.

Wasn't a cushioned shoe timeless for running on pavement? We knew from customer feedback and letters over the years that shoes had literally "saved" people by allowing them to run. We witnessed hundreds of stories on how the Adrenaline GTS, the Beast, or the Addiction shoes had allowed people to run pain-free. But the new stories on barefoot and minimalist shoes leading to pain-free running were equally compelling and no doubt true. Could they both be right?

My intuition said yes. Every specialty run shop knew, after fitting hundreds of feet in a good week, that no two runners are exactly alike. And yet, we had no clinical studies that addressed the shoe/no-shoe debate with real data. No one did, including the barefoot zealots. The data didn't exist; just beliefs and opinions. We resolved to get that data from defendable clinical studies. After all, there should be one truth on the mechanics of human motion, running, and the right shoe. If we did not come with credible answers, the whole category would be suspect with multiple versions of the truth.

→ Customer Obsession + Insight Drives Innovation

This was a watershed moment for Brooks's leadership. While the industry zagged to meet consumer trend, Brooks zigged to anchor itself in research, data, facts, and insights.

The barefoot trend presented Brooks with the opportunity to reinvent performance running. (Injuries from the barefoot experiment and lawsuits began to rise, with Vibram subject to class-action lawsuits on injury claims.) The running world was looking for thought leadership and innovation grounded in facts. At this time at Brooks, we lacked a long-term vision, or what Jim Collins calls a Big Hairy Audacious Goal (BHAG). It didn't help that we tended to be self-critical. At an offsite one day, we diagnosed our brand as safe but a little boring. Brooks was likened to a Volvo car or the Olive Garden restaurant. But during that same session, our advertising agency presented a challenge on thought leadership. They flashed a slide with a passage frequently attributed to cultural anthropologist Margaret Mead: "Never doubt that a small group of thoughtful, committed citizens can change the world. Indeed, it is the only thing that ever has."

It was meant to inspire, which it did. But it also read like marching orders for us. We had to commit to innovation and be willing to take risks.

Two Brooks colleagues would play key roles in solving the shoe/no-shoe question for Brooks and, in many ways, for the industry: Carson Caprara, a former University of Colorado runner, and Pete Humphrey, a former soccer player.

While recovering from injuries in college, Carson spent years grinding on the retail floors of Boulder Running Company in Colorado and later in his hometown of Austin, Texas, at RunTex. Both retail stores were part of inventing the specialty run shop, places where runners convened to talk about what was and wasn't working in their training and their gear.

Pete arrived at Brooks having refined his skills working with Premier League players while at Pentland Sports, the parent company of Reebok, in the United Kingdom. Carson and Pete were two sides of the same coin. Carson brought runner insights from deep research as well as a studied philosophy to running shoe concepts and designs. Pete understood the biomechanics and engineering to deliver breakthrough product that performed as intended.

Together, Carson and Pete began to reframe the sudden "less is more" shoe fad to an insightful conversation around both the unique mechanics of motion and the different run experiences runners crave. This focus on each person's unique motion and desired run experience would become foundational to Brooks's future.

As the barefoot craze got underway, we began working on a minimalist line of shoes. Product development was well down the path, but we were uncertain how to position the line. Brooks was approached by the human-centered product design firm IDEO. IDEO eventually convinced us to engage it to mine for runner insights on how to position our new minimalist-inspired product line. IDEO has designed everything from high-tech medical equipment to the first Apple mouse, Nike sunglasses, and the squishy handle on your toothbrush.

The investment was large for Brooks. The key was not just getting an answer to this one barefoot question but teaching our team how to "fish" for runner insights on our own. IDEO agreed to embed Carson and other Brooks people in their research team. I wanted our team to learn from the best and spread that mindset and approach throughout our organization.

→ Insight: The Barefoot Boom Was Not About the Shoe

Now embedded with IDEO in the San Francisco Bay Area, Carson embraced the firm's principle that designers must learn from empathy. IDEO does everything it can to eliminate bias from research. One afternoon Carson walked past an IDEO conference room and paused briefly to take notice of some words scrawled on the whiteboard: "Runners feel disenfranchised from their shoe purchase."

Specialty run retailers are like raccoons. They will pick apart a shoe to find its flaws. If it fits long or short or doesn't flex right on the foot, they won't pull it out of the stock room. Instead, they will ship it right back to us. No one is a greater advocate for runners than specialty running stores.

However, Carson and IDEO were finding that runners felt they had to take whatever pill was prescribed. They felt ill prepared and therefore vulnerable to the advice they heard from a friend, coach, magazine, or whoever happened to be on the showroom floor that day. What runners were hungry for was independent research about how their personal biomechanics translated to the right shoe for the run they wanted to have.

The light bulb flashed on. Carson discerned a difference between runners who want to float through their run and those who want to feel their run. "I want to be high from the ground and not feel a thing underfoot," or "I want to be low to the ground and tuned in to my terrain." Our customers were telling us it mattered to them how the shoe felt on the foot and during the run. The approach to organize our products into experience was born: Float and Feel.

→ Committing to Research-Driven Design

Back at headquarters, we pored over the data to distill insights and formulate a plan. I was stunned by the conversation that *Born to Run* had created without any real clinical research behind the barefoot claims. In the vacuum of research-based thought leadership, we stepped forward. We decided to invest aggressively in research and development of the mechanics of human motion, running, and injury. We partnered with two world-class university research programs and funded clinical studies. We would then commit to build our product on the foundation of the latest biomechanical research, technology, and analytics.

One of the first expressions of this approach came in the form of an open letter I sent to runners worldwide and to our industry. We stood alone in confronting the barefoot phenomenon.

An Open Letter to the Running Community

For many of us, running is an inseparable part of our lives—we need it. When we run, we improve our health, relieve stress, achieve personal goals, compete, raise money, and have fun. On any given weekend, check out a running event in any city across the globe and you'll be inspired by runners spanning ages, speeds, motivations, and goals—each with their own stories. At Brooks, inspiring everyone to run and be active is our reason for being.

Given the passion felt about our sport, it's easy to understand how everything about the run is actively studied, critiqued, debated, and questioned—including shoes. People strive to run faster, longer, healthier, more efficiently, and injury-free mile after mile, and they've traditionally looked to their footwear to deliver that. But many people have recently questioned whether running barefoot is better, so we feel it's time for Brooks to join the public dialogue.

Let's call a spade a spade. We make running shoes—high-quality, biomechanically mapped, performance running shoes calibrated for runners' unique needs. We hope runners buy our shoes and we're confident they'll enjoy them. But this isn't about selling shoes. And, quite frankly, this isn't even about running barefoot.

So what are we talking about here? First and foremost, we're all talking about running, and that's a great thing because we believe to our core that running is a positive force in our world. We want everyone to run and be happy. But to get there, whether you should run barefoot is not the great debate. We are all unique. The focus should be on how you run and train, and then finding the right shoe that addresses your unique biomechanical needs. The Perfect Ride for Every Stride, as we say at Brooks. Let's look at a snapshot of the running population:

At one end of the spectrum, we know there are runners who lack foot strength leading to severe pronation. They may strike heavily and need a great deal of support to run injury- and pain-free. We hear repeatedly from them that the Brooks Beast "saved their lives."

At the other end of the spectrum are the biomechanically blessed (and/or conditioned through training) who have naturally healthy gaits and enjoy great efficiency. These gazelles may wear shoes, they may not.

The vast majority of runners (including this middle-of-the-packer!) fall in between. And for us, we strongly believe most of our mileage should be logged in a performance running shoe, not barefoot. For us, supportive, cushioned footwear is not only beneficial, it also plays an essential role in delivering a comfortable, injury-free running experience.

The open letter created a thought leadership moment for Brooks. It brought attention to a more in-depth white paper, a carefully researched and passionately argued case for biomechanics in shoe design. We pointed out that there was no conclusive evidence demonstrating barefoot or minimalist running reduces injury or that running in running shoes causes injury in every runner. What the data clearly showed was that knee injuries have long been the most prevalent among runners. This fact led our shift from a hyper-focus on the ankle and overpronation to the knee and movements such as internal tibial rotation and knee abduction/adduction. We discovered that the body's number-one priority when running was to keep the knee stable and moving in its preferred motion pathway. As a result, motion at the foot and ankle could not be looked at in isolation and may in fact be beneficial to maintaining knee stability. This was a major paradigm shift from the conventional thinking that all foot overpronation was a bad thing.

We were systematically building a world-class research-and-development organization that included relationships with some of the world's top academic institutions and biomechanists. Our commitment was to find truths on those combinations of upper body movements, footfall patterns, gaits, body masses, and foot shapes—in other words, how you run. All of that matters and, like signatures, every runner is different. This enables us to assess how you move and then produce shoes that keep you in your habitual motion path, the natural motion that works best for your joints. Doubling down on biomechanics was good for customers and good for our industry.

We have a hundred thousand runners in our wear tester database. From prototypes to final sample shoes, we gather feedback through observations, qualitative interviews, and readings from machines, treadmills, on location, and fellow race competitors. For the latter real-world field testing, we typically execute three rounds of wear testing on every new style. For each round, the shoe is slightly adjusted to hit a desired fit, feel, and ride profile. Samples are shipped to between twenty and thirty-two runners per round; wear testers put in a minimum number of miles and then answer three robust surveys throughout a defined testing period. We get honest and colorful feedback from our wear testers. They know shoes and can detect even the slightest imperfections. This program is expensive and time consuming in our product development cycle. It is also the only way to deliver consistent fit, feel, and ride. Many consultants and financial experts look at the program and salivate over the "efficiencies" to be had in eliminating it. But it has become an essential advantage in delivering the consistent fit that runners expect.

Lab testing had been important to me early in my tenure at Brooks. We made the decision to bring our lab in-house to create more hands-on shared learning across the product team. We bought our first treadmill, but only had floor space for it in the copy-machine room. We got serious about biomechanical research, ultimately creating a state-of-the-art running lab. We brought on leading researchers to study every runner's "signature," which is an individual's unique running form defined by their body's habitual motion path. The task of modern running shoes should be to help runners stay within their unique motion corridor at all times. We're obsessed with every parameter of your run, but none more so than pronation and its impact on bones, tendons, and ligaments. We're not interested in matching runners to shoes. We want shoes to match runners. Our view is that everyone has a Natural Habitual Joint Motion (NHJM), which is your body's path of least resistance. Our job is to make *your* shoe, not someone else's. We make the shoe that helps keep you on your path.

→ Clinical Insight: Each Runner Has an Individual Run Signature

The results from these investments were so important, in fact, that we continued to build thought leadership. Brooks published a provocative paper detailing its Run Signature philosophy that was widely circulated throughout the industry. Run Signature remains a revolutionary point of view, yet it is based on years of scientific research. Iain Hunter, a biomechanist at Brigham Young University, studied the footfall of each of the twenty-four runners competing in the 10K finals in the 2012 Olympic Team Trials held at the University of Oregon. He placed a high-speed camera on the side of the track to capture those footfalls and then analyze them side by side. You might expect these elite-level runners, all proven capable of finishing a 10K within a minute of one another, to have similar form. Not so. Each runner strikes the ground in a unique way. Each runner has his or her own personal stride, like a fingerprint.

Dr. Iain Hunter of the BYU Biomechanics Lab captured the foot strikes of Men's 10K competitors in the 2012 US Olympic Team Trials. Like a signature or fingerprint, each runner leaves his or her own personal mark of individuality on the track. These findings informed Brooks's Run Signature philosophy that the only "right" way to run is the way your body naturally wants to move. *Courtesy of Iain Hunter*

One's Run Signature becomes the new baseline or starting point from which we define each runner's optimal form and alignment. Our research led us to believe the answer to reducing injuries, enhancing comfort, and improving performance is not to fix a runner's "flaws," but to work with the natural and highly individual motion paths of the joints. The focus then becomes keeping the runner in this path of least resistance for as long as possible during a run. Perturbations such as shoe geometries, midsole hardness, or excessive stabilizing technologies can push some runners outside of their preferred motion path. The task of modern running shoes should be to help these runners stay within their unique motion corridor at all times. By maintaining these habitual motion patterns and the shoe's harmony with the way the body wants to move, the runner optimizes muscle activity and joint motion, reducing the onset of fatigue and form breakdown.

Throughout this research, Carson, Pete, and their teams got to know runners on a personal level. Insights can come from anywhere. Rather than build a shoe they thought people wanted, then selling it and determining if it works, they built those insights into shoe design at every stage. Their approach was: How do we scope it for the runner, and then scale it into a franchise model?

To be successful, we calculated that we'd need an investment of $10 million. That meant I would have to convince our owners at Fruit of the Loom back in Bowling Green, Kentucky, that we were right. We went to the mat to advocate our point of view. We agreed to shrink our profit plan by half and invest marketing dollars to ensure a future based on doing what's right for runners and running.

In October 2011, Brooks launched the PureProject footwear collection, a lightweight ride with a sock-like feel that met the demands of runners inspired by the barefoot running concept but now better informed about their biomechanics. The collection, comprising four styles, was categorized as minimalist but with the support you'd want for running on a trail, a gravel road, or even on asphalt. Moreover, these first-ever minimalist styles from Brooks addressed the run experience some runners craved: a closer-to-ground, connected ride. PureProject delivered on the insight that the barefoot phenomenon was really not about the shoe, but about a close-to-the-ground "feel" experience.

Our investment in biomechanics also resulted in a competitive edge over those brands that chased after barefoot. Better understanding of what runners wanted and expected at that time resulted in a three- to six-month lead in product line development. With the introduction of PureProject, Brooks immediately grabbed 33 percent market share within the minimalist running shoe category.

I was quoted in *Running Insight,* an industry news source, as saying that if you want to live your life with a "less is more" philosophy, I can understand that. But when it comes to a performance product, the idea that "less is more" is absolute crap. In something as important as your daily run or a long-distance race, the assertion that "less is more" was simply wrong. We were resonating with runners, something I could not have said several years earlier.

Our new muscle in mining and synthesizing biomechanical data and runner feedback drove improvements to other shoes in our existing footwear line. We perfected the Ghost, about which *Runner's World* test editor Amanda Furrer wrote, "I could wax poetic," which is why in 2020 it was honored with its eleventh Editors' Choice Award from the magazine.

We were not just managing a business or a brand, we were creating one. We were pushing the envelope on product by testing, testing, and retesting everything, including our own assumptions. And we were having fun. A reporter at the time wrote that we took running shoes very seriously, though not at the risk of having a good time.

→ Brooks's Battle Cry: Run Happy

When I arrived at Brooks, the company had a way to describe its culture, which was captured by the tagline, "Run Happy." It fit this merry band of runners who worked hard, ran hard, enjoyed the journey, and celebrated the post-run results.

But the idea ran far deeper. Run Happy celebrates the healing positivity of what the run brings to your life. It delivers something, or you wouldn't return to run the next day or the next week. You won't always feel happiness in the midst of that hill or on a bad day, but afterward you are going to feel the runner's high, whatever that may mean for you.

Run Happy may be best expressed in a statement we published at the time.

Run Happy Is . . .

Everything we are and all that we value can be summarized by just two words: **Run Happy.**

But when we say, "**Run Happy,**" what do we really mean? What is **Run Happy?**

Run Happy is not just a tagline . . . or a market position . . . or a slogan.

Run Happy is the emotional core of the running experience.

Run Happy is a feeling, an attitude, a spirit that lives in the hearts and minds of all runners—young or old, fast or slow, male or female, master or newbie.

Run Happy is each runner's deep and meaningful love of running.

And because of that, **Run Happy** is feeling . . .

- Powerful
- Connected
- Passionate
- Energized
- Fast
- Peaceful
- Ecstatic
- Committed
- Free
- Unstoppable

Run Happy is . . .

- Passing the runner up ahead of you
- In touch with something deep within
- A high five with a complete stranger
- Morning's first light on your favorite trail

Run Happy is the best part of the runner's day, the part that understands that the worst day spent running is better than the best day at the office.

When we tap into Run Happy, we celebrate this thing we and all runners love.

The words Run Happy remind runners everywhere why they fell in love with running in the first place.

That is why Run Happy is . . .

- Our battle cry
- Our flag in the ground
- The tip of our spear

That is what Run Happy is.

And that is why Run Happy is Brooks.

→ Bringing the Run Happy Ethos to Runners

If you've ever run or observed a Rock 'n' Roll Marathon, you know what happy running looks like. Established in 1998 in San Diego, Rock 'n' Roll offers full and half marathon races in cities around the world. The event has attracted many first-time racers. It's the original festival run. Along the course, runners are entertained by live bands and rock-themed water stations, all in a party-like atmosphere. There's even a live concert at the finish line.

While attending a Fleet Feet conference in 2009, I learned that the Rock 'n' Roll Marathon Series footwear sponsor, New Balance, was exiting. This was a huge opportunity at a fortuitous moment. About 40 percent of Rock 'n' Roll's half-million runners were first-time race participants. Imagine race corrals full of new, passionate runners who will forever remember this monumental experience for which they'd trained for months. As a brand, we could be present and attach to those memories in a positive way. We jumped on the opportunity and in September 2009 announced a multiyear deal with Rock 'n' Roll. My excitement in the resulting news coverage was palpable. I told reporters we couldn't wait to run alongside so many avid, inspiring runners by supporting their ambitions to run longer, farther, and faster.

Rock 'n' Roll gave us the advantage of accelerating the expression of Brooks's Run Happy spirit. It wouldn't be just a race sponsorship with us writing a check to put up banners. We would activate and engage runners at every opportunity from sign-up, packet pickup, expo, and the race. While competing brands were pulling back amid the recession and a barefoot movement, we went big and got loud and proud. These events would become a canvas where Brooks's marketing vice president, Dave Larson, would bring Run Happy alive for hundreds of thousands of runners in a manner only Brooks could pull off.

The Brooks booth became a must-see inside the Rock 'n' Roll exhibition hall. One year we built a stage to resemble a nineteenth-century Ringling Bros. and Barnum & Bailey Circus, complete with an old-fashioned carnival barker. We called it the Cavalcade of Curiosities. One curiosity was a skit involving "the human Jesus Lizard," a person dressed like the reptile that generates such momentum as to run across stretches of water. In the midst of the stage, we created a vat of cornstarch-based fluid to mimic the Brooks DNA midsole technology, which was non-Newtonian in its physical properties.

DNA was a truly breakthrough technology for Brooks and is in all our shoes to this day. When force is applied, DNA midsole material instantaneously firms up at the molecular level so you can transition from heel strike to toe-off with propulsion off a firm surface. Too soft and it is like running on a pillow or sand; you will needlessly lose speed. DNA gives Brooks shoes a soft first feel in the store, dampens impact on heel strike, and then firms up to create a base to push off of to your next stride. It was highly engineered at the molecular level, a running-specific midsole that was truly the engine, chassis, and transmission of our running shoes. Runners could feel it.

The Jesus Lizard (and crowd volunteers) ran across our springy layer of cornstarch (another non-Newtonian material) to cheers from runners and their families. There were games, a fortune teller, and lots of product to choose from. Our booth even included an old, dilapidated bus we retrofitted into a functioning vehicle with capsules inside that entertained event-goers while educating them on gear technologies, runner maladies, and Brooks's history. When not at a Rock 'n' Roll event, we took the Brooks Cavalcade of Curiosities bus on a national tour to engage runners at specialty running stores.

At events and throughout much of our marketing, we called this approach *adver-edu-tainment*: part advertising, part education, part entertainment. It was unique in our industry and resonated well with many runners, especially those who found running hard or intimidating. It gave most a positive brand impression that stuck.

We built another marathon expo booth to look like a giant bowl of pasta, a favorite meal among runners. At the Chicago Marathon, we debuted a booth that was skinned like a M*A*S*H unit, only we called it B*R*A*S*H, for "Brooks Running Athlete Support Hospital." Under our tent we offered gait analysis, talked about biomechanics and shoe technologies, helped runners try on gear, and answered any questions they had about training and their game plan for the race. They may have been able to get the same information from other brands on the expo floor, but we wrapped everything in a fun, welcoming, celebratory way. Though Brooks was not the title sponsor of this event, expo participant surveys showed Brooks was the brand they remembered most. The entire experience exuded both Run Happy and Brooks taking our product seriously, but not always ourselves.

→ Performance Product + Run Happy = $1 Billion Idea

I remained convinced that Brooks's opportunity in premium performance run was big. Plus, our Run Happy positioning was novel and unique. Given the size of the category, we had a billion-dollar idea. I was certain that Brooks could become the next billion-dollar brand in running. I also felt strongly that we had to wake up the industry, including the most influential retailers, to see Brooks as a brand rather than just a source of a few good shoes. Brooks's communications director, Tamara Hills, and I decided to announce its potential during a press tour. We created a strategy presentation on Brooks's opportunity to "Own the Run" by 2020, but we neglected to give a heads-up to executives inside the company that we planned to quantify our vision with a "B" number. Over the course of two days in the spring of 2010, we briefed media, retailers, and influencers on this $1 billion vision. The setting was a newly opened luxury residential building on Lenox Hill in New York City. The owners offered the space at no cost, because they wanted to align the residences with health and wellness. The building's gym allowed Carson and team to show off our Run Signature approach with gait analyses for attendees. CBS, *Fitness, Good Housekeeping, Men's Journal, Teen Vogue,* and dozens more joined us. Headlines began to pop. "Brooks Running for a Billion," and "Run Baby, Run." The *New York Times* picked up on the story, explaining to readers that creative, inclusive marketing was reaching beyond Brooks's core audience by putting the fun in run. As story after story appeared, I was pleased that we had executed a very public market signaling event, planting the Brooks flag firmly in performance and engaging with runners in a unique way.

Back at the office, however, I began to hear anxious reverberations from the team.

A billion? Is he crazy?

In retrospect, I should have warned my executive team I was going to publicly declare our billion-dollar idea for Brooks. But after the shock wore off and headlines calmed down, my team realized this vision was aligned with Brooks's core strengths. While running is a unique, deeply personal experience that belongs to each runner, we had a shared business mindset to "Own the Run." My public proclamation was simply an outcome of the game we were already playing. And we were in this game to win. I wanted the world to know we were going after it and they should expect more from us.

This was not the first time I'd worked with Tamara. Given her role, we partnered regularly on internal and executive communications efforts. Just a couple months prior, upon her return to work from maternity leave, she helped me write our open letter to runners and our Run Signature white paper. But now it was time to figure out how we were going to articulate Run Happy to more people, and I needed her help. A communications pro, runner, and longtime employee, Tamara was the perfect person to help us express and deepen the meaning of Run Happy. At its core, Run Happy was and always has been a celebration of your run and no one else's, no matter if you're a first-time runner slogging through your initial mile or you just set a personal record in your thirtieth marathon. In a focus group during this time, we asked participants why they ran. One working, single mother of two teenage boys said, "Each day, my run is my gift from me to me." I'll never forget the powerful clarity I found in her response. The role her run played in her life was huge, and Brooks had an opportunity to help keep her on that path. Our Run Happy promise honored and celebrated what drew each runner to the run and then helped make their next run better than their last. It was about

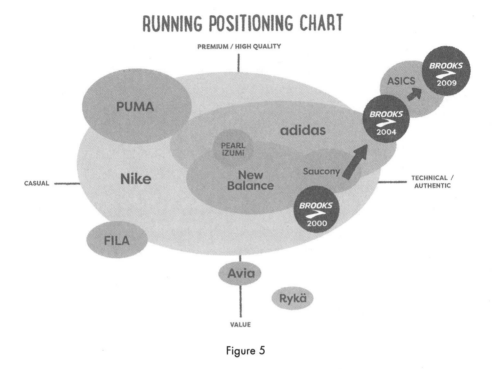

Figure 5

inspiration to find your best Run Happy every day, not about an aspirational podium promise. We pushed off the big platform brands with this energy and believed it was a winning differentiator in our space.

To pinpoint where we were (and wanted to be) in the minds of customers, we worked to plot our brand positioning relative to others (see figure 5). Initially, it was more of a rational product analysis with "casual versus technical/authentic" on the x axis and "premium/high quality versus value/pricing" on the y axis. Brooks was on a mission to lead the upper right quadrant: premium, high-quality, technical, and authentic.

To be a real brand, let alone a loved brand, we needed to stretch beyond a cerebral connection with the customer. I strongly believed that great brands connect with minds and hearts at both a rational and emotional level. In most categories and certainly in performance running gear, product is purchased on a rational level, based primarily on an individual's needs. If the product works, trust follows. But when runners choose to wear and then become loyal to a brand, that's when you know they've moved beyond rational trust into emotional attachment. They wear a specific brand not just because it works, but because it says something to the world about who they are. They might share the brand's values, or the brand reminds them of the positive emotions triggering why they do what they do, for example, run. The mind and the heart. Brooks has this inherent tension in our performance products, culture, and brand. We've often thought the right archetypes for our brand are the sage and the jester. The best performance product in the world for your brain, and a celebration of the afterglow and positive energy you get from a great run for your heart—that's Run Happy.

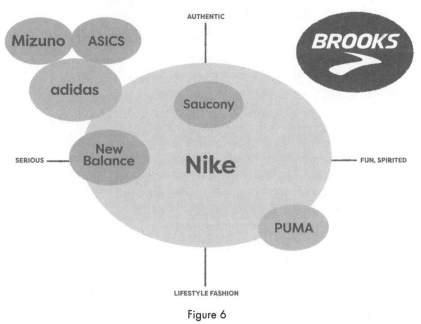

BROOKS BRAND POSITIONING

Figure 6

With a refocused lens, we drew a new framework (see figure 6). This time, we measured brands on attributes of "serious versus fun, spirited" and "authentic versus lifestyle." We wanted to be alone in the upper right quadrant: the best product plus an inclusive, relatable brand that was runner to runner, fun and authentic.

→ Running Is Too Big to Be Owned by Just One Brand

Brooks's Run Happy positioning came into view at the 2012 US Olympic Team Trials for Track and Field on the University of Oregon's campus in Eugene. This was the home field for the legendary Steve Prefontaine and is also well known for its close ties with Nike and its founders.

Brooks invited dozens of our closest retail partners to join us at the trials. We rented a fraternity house for lodging, hired a chef, and planned events including fun run meetups each morning. Before heading down to Eugene, our sales and marketing team proposed the idea of hiring a small prop plane to fly a "Run Happy" banner above Hayward Field during the competition to cheer on the athletes. Nike, of course, had a tight lock on trials sponsorship, including a twenty-seven-year deal with USA Track & Field, but it didn't own the airspace. Rick Wilhelm, head of sales for specialty stores; Jesse Williams, head of sports marketing; and I got up Saturday morning and took our guests to the competition at the field. We all got through security and found our seats in the sold-out stadium. Then we got set to watch the fastest athletes in America compete for spots on Team USA for the 2012 London games. It was great to see the airplane and our banner circling the stadium on a perfect sunny day.

It was also clearly attracting Nike's attention. There were huddles near the track, and we noticed a Nike marketing guy had the ear of a marketing director for USA Track & Field.

Nike was clearly not happy with us. The marketing director marched up the bleachers and began to yell at us, "I said no guerilla marketing at the trials!" That night, we discussed at length if we should fly the plane the next day. We had our pilots clear it with the FAA to make sure it was all legal. We even got off-the-record feedback from USA Track & Field officials who encouraged us to keep flying it.

The conclusion on whether to cheer on the athletes with "Run Happy"? Hell, yes!

And so on Sunday we did it again. This time, another plane (I assume it was Nike's) took to the skies above Hayward Field and successfully nudged our own plane and Run Happy banner farther from the competition. The marketing director returned for more animated discussions along with Nike people and security, and this time they asked us all to leave. Since we had paid full price for our tickets, we asked why and on what basis

Brooks charters a prop plane to fly a "Run Happy" banner over competitors and fans during the 2012 US Olympic Team Trials for Track and Field at the University of Oregon's Hayward Field. *Courtesy of Jess Lyons*

they were kicking us out. The answer was on the back of the tickets. They were only a "license to attend" that could be revoked at any time for any reason. And so they were revoked. Rick, Jesse, and I volunteered to leave so our guests could remain and enjoy the competition. We walked out to the beer garden and watched the remaining events from a distance.

We had poked the bear.

The pivot to experience-driven product design empowered by Run Signature and insights research, plus our Run Happy brand positioning, unleashed phenomenal growth for Brooks over the next several years (see figure 7). We became the fastest growing brand in running, passing Asics in November 2010 to become number one in market share in the specialty run channel, a lofty goal we had set nine years earlier. If you don't lead in specialty

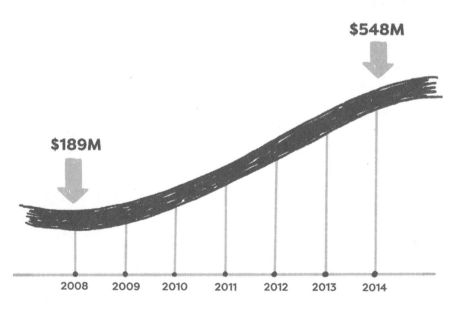

GLOBAL REVENUE

2008 — INVEST TO LEAD OUTCOME

$548M

$189M

| 2008 | 2009 | 2010 | 2011 | 2012 | 2013 | 2014 |

Figure 7

run stores like Fleet Feet, Super Jock 'n Jill, Gazelle Sports, Luke's Locker, Playmakers, Pacers, Run N Fun, Marathon Sports, and Road Runner, you will never lead with runners. We tripled our US footwear business in five years by adding new runners to our brand.

Celebrating milestones is part of our culture. On the morning we learned we'd surpassed Asics, we gathered employees in our lunchroom, told them to quickly wrap up what they were working on, and invited them all to meet us at Redhook Brewery outside of Seattle near our headquarters, for what turned into a long day of toasts and shared pride in our accomplishment.

We had come so far. With growth came space constraints at our current headquarters in Bothell, Washington, and our lease was coming to term. A reporter at the *New York Times* wrote that our "growing army of designers, product managers, customer service representatives and marketing gurus needed a more spacious workplace." We needed to find a new home for Brooks, and so we began to investigate a long list of potential headquarters sites.

Generally speaking, the greater Seattle market is split in two by Lake Washington, creating what locals call the Eastside and Westside. Brooks employees lived on both sides of Lake Washington, and points north and south. I quickly found out that when it comes to preferred office location, people vote by zip code, so I knew I had to own this decision. By this time, Tamara Hills had shifted roles to work alongside me in my office. The first special project I engaged her in was managing our global headquarters search. We considered more than forty spaces, and on a solo run around Lake Union, I carefully weighed the options. I chose a site just north of downtown Seattle on the shores of Lake Union and along King County's scenic Burke-Gilman Trail, a twenty-seven-mile rails-to-trails path that links the city's Eastside and Westside.

The actual building didn't yet exist; the site at the time was a tired surface parking lot next to a city dump. Yet I could envision our opportunity to engage and, I hoped, inspire the thousands of runners and active people who use the beloved Burke daily. Having a store where we could interact with runners daily checked a box from the original IDEO research, and this location sat right on the trail. It also offered a far more compelling scenario for recruiting talent. Ultimately, I signed a deal on a pile of dirt and a dream to plant our brand flag and grow our team in Seattle. Our new building would hit deep green standards and surpass Leadership in Energy and Environmental Design (LEED) Platinum certification in sustainability, something that mattered to our employees and to our customers. We felt Brooks deserved to be known and respected among other strong, innovative Seattle-area brands including Amazon, Microsoft, REI, Alaska Airlines, Boeing, and Starbucks. We had the opportunity to be on the map as Seattle's running brand.

In February 2013, just a week or two after breaking ground for the new building construction, Brooks's employees organized an eighteen-mile relay run from our previous headquarters in Bothell to Gas Works Park, located just a quarter mile via the Burke-Gilman Trail from what would become our new global headquarters with a flagship retail store, Brooks Trailhead. I told everyone it didn't matter if they ran fast or slow, one mile or the whole race. Just run happy. And they did. It was chaotic, hilarious, and consistent with our culture. Our baton was a mini replica of the Seattle Space Needle. We gathered at our finish point in the park, standing underneath a massive race event inflatable with the iconic landmark in view.

2014 marked the hundredth anniversary of the Brooks brand, so in May we brought retailers, industry partners, media, and other VIPs to Seattle for a symposium, another fun relay race, and one hell of a party. *Runner's World* editor-in-chief David Willey told the *Seattle Times*, "Runners can trust [Brooks] and to do that on top of where they were—all the ups and downs that they've had—it is a testament to their product."

That year Brooks surpassed a half-billion dollars in revenue. But becoming a billion-dollar brand, I learned, would require adding a sixth leadership principle to my manifesto:

1. **Own a Niche:** Pursue greatness by simultaneously owning a niche, growing, and delivering premium profits, consistently and over time.

2. **Build a Moat:** Create a distinctive, defendable brand proposition. Getting credit for it from the customer (at full price) is the measure of its strength and essential to sustainable success.

3. **Solve for Profitability:** Engineer it into your business model. If successful, it can create a flywheel of investment to strengthen your moat.

4. **Vision without Execution Is Hallucination:** Dreams and plans are meaningless if they're not backed by action. Walk the talk.

5. **Lead Authentically:** Focus, curiosity, and trust are foundational to connecting with people. Treat them with respect, integrity, and humility.

6. **The Ultimate Advantage Is a Strong Culture.**

We were well on our way to that billion-dollar vision. Our dedication to running-only withstood the economic headwinds of the Great Recession and the aftershocks of a barefoot running earthquake.

Through those ups and downs, Brooks also endured a parade of owners. We were now part of the Berkshire Hathaway family, and Brooks would soon welcome one of our biggest fans, Warren Buffett, to a renewed, reenergized brand.

PART II

‒ ‒ ‒ ‒ ‒ ‒ ‒ ‒ ‒ ‒ →

CHAPTER 6

Meeting the
Oracle of Omaha

JUST AFTER NEW YEAR'S DAY 2012, I returned to the office from the holiday break to find a voicemail message from Warren Buffett. He said he had an idea he wanted to run past me. I had been on email throughout the break, but kicked myself for not checking voicemail. *Ugh*—I had let a voicemail from Warren Buffett sit for *five days!* I returned the call immediately, and Warren wanted to know how much integration Brooks had with our parent company, Fruit of the Loom, which was owned by Berkshire Hathaway.

"To what extent are you dependent on Fruit? Are you sharing any services or systems?"

The answer, as he suspected, was not much. Other than legal and insurance, Brooks was independent. In fact, Fruit of the Loom probably thought of us as the crazy uncle out in Seattle.

In my view, Berkshire Hathaway is a unique business model and culture among the Fortune 500. It is an insurance company with an investment portfolio of both owned and partially owned businesses welded together. Famously, they buy a company and let it run with complete independence. Warren Buffett, Vice

Chairman Charlie Munger, and the corporate staff of around twenty-five people truly believe in autonomy and decentralization as the path to maximizing value over time. As part of the Russell Group within Fruit of the Loom, Brooks was tucked two corporate levels below Buffett, but we generated results that caught his attention. A Berkshire Hathaway watcher, Lawrence A. Cunningham, author of *Berkshire Beyond Buffett: The Enduring Value of Values,* wrote that as a rule of thumb, shoe companies are worth twice sales. This made Brooks as valuable alone as what Berkshire paid for Russell Athletic and its holdings when it was merged into Fruit.

That January day when we spoke, Warren told me he had been thinking that Brooks should become a direct subsidiary. He felt that Fruit needed to focus on apparel, and we had opportunities to continue to grow in footwear as a running brand. Stunned and ecstatic, I went on to tell Warren how strong Brooks results were in 2011 and that our momentum for the coming year was solid.

He laughed. "That is great," he said. "From here on out, I will be taking credit for Brooks's success, too!"

When I walked out of my office after the call, I could hardly contain my excitement. What a way to start the year. And I had yet to fully understand the advantages that Warren's personal support would bring.

My career to that point had included crash courses in various ownership groups. I had been exposed to a gamut of ownership structures and investors, including private companies, public companies, venture capital, captured companies, and private capital pools. I'd seen the good, the bad, and the ugly. What I learned is that if you were in the long-term brand-building business, it was critical to understand the investors' objectives. What were their expectations for returns on their investment?

Money always has an agenda, and no one captured this sentiment better than native Minnesotan and Nobel Prize winner

Bob Dylan in his epic song recorded in 1965 "It's Alright, Ma (I'm Only Bleeding)" in which he refers to money's ability to actually curse.

Dylan's lyrics echoed in my brain as I toiled for owners and investors. Money doesn't whisper hopes and dreams in your ear. It expects, assumes, demands, and, yes, when provoked may even curse at you. Money has an agenda, always. Failure to understand money puts you, as a leader, in peril.

Owners or investors may have a short-term horizon. They need to fix it fast or polish it up to sell the business. Some might want to show as little profit as possible to minimize the taxes they owe. Others will cut every cost and initiative possible to drive near-term profits without regard to future earning power. I have seen investors on a mission to remedy disputes and slights, operating on an emotional level, ignoring business realities and opportunities. I've witnessed so-called investors behave as the traders they truly are, seeking events where they can arbitrage short-term profits from mispriced assets. Since my Pillsbury experience, I have come to believe that pretty much anyone can cut costs to show a profit. It is not rocket science. The real challenge is to create double-digit growth and premium profitability, simultaneously and consistently over time. That is where real value is created. Fortunately, some owners have a longer time horizon and understand that future financial results will be driven by customers responding to a brand and being willing to pay full value for their products and services. They see financial opportunity and value in building a brand over time.

→ Solving for Your Company's Investors

Since 2001 when I joined Brooks, we have had four different owners. In each case, I took responsibility for both soliciting and earning their support for the team to pursue the opportunities we saw to build the brand. Syncing up the nonowner CEO's strategy with the investor's objectives is a puzzle to be solved. Investors bring an agenda that includes a set of goals. And of course the CEO also has a set of goals that reflect the opportunities in the business. Ideally there is critical overlap in all the right areas, but that's not always the case. I learned the hard way to be acutely aware of the investors' goals, constraints, pressures, philosophies, style, values, and structure. It is essential to know the agenda of the money backing your business.

Along my career journey, I have experienced a variety of ownership structures and approaches. Observing and learning why each behaved, operated, and arrived at the decisions it did has made me a better CEO. The widely varying approaches may present initially as mere style, but as I thought more deeply about it, I came to understand that the drivers are much more complex and innate to who they are.

→ The Private Company: The Owner Sets the Agenda

As a junior banker at Norwest Bank, I bought into Milton Friedman's 1970 *New York Times* essay "The Social Responsibility of Business Is to Increase Its Profits" and the premise that businesses existed to make money. I was twenty-three years old, just out of college, and I managed an eclectic menagerie of mid-market loans. We regularly reviewed updated company financial statements on one of my loans, so the loan committee sent me out to better understand a local business. The owner had shared an income statement with us, but would not give us a balance sheet. We secured most loans with inventory and receivables, so a current balance sheet was a given. If the company doesn't make money, inventory and receivables would be the collateral we would have to collect on the loan. I visited the business to get the balance sheet so we'd have a fuller picture.

I was persistent but polite and professional. It was becoming clear the owner was extremely reluctant to share a balance sheet. He was practically sweating when he finally gave it to me, and for good reason. He had been using aggressive inventory accounting for years to lower his reported profit and taxes. I had never imagined the possibility of "negative inventory" but that is what he reported. His goal was to avoid taxes. And that he did. Things worked out on the loan (as we could count millions in inventory despite what was on the books) but this was the start of my appreciation for investor motivations and the impact on a business.

→ ## The Public Company: Tyranny of the Quarter

A few years later at Pillsbury, a large-cap public growth company in the go-go 1980s, I learned about the tyranny of quarterly earnings: the forced march of top- and bottom-line growth every three months. When blessed with a high multiple on your stock, Wall Street demands growth, which can create powerful incentives to engineer results at the expense of longer-term success. I witnessed firsthand the perils of chasing sales and cutting spending to hit financial targets versus investing and innovating for the customer. Across dozens of businesses, I saw systematic underinvestment in products and marketing. When the music stopped, they hit a wall and were taken over.

Delivering against numerical goals and expectations set by people who do not understand the business is satisfying until you fall short. I came to believe the practice was on the verge of being unethical. Shame on the CEO who delivers in the short-term at the expense of tomorrow. I've been hardwired with this conviction since high school. When I attended Boys State in the 1970s, we all went to see Andrew Lloyd Webber and Tim Rice's musical *Joseph and the Amazing Technicolor Dreamcoat* at American University in Washington, D.C. The music is great, and its lesson of playing the long game stuck with me.

Joseph has a dream about seven fat cows, seven skinny cows, seven healthy ears of corn, and seven dead ears of corn. He concludes that there will be seven plentiful years of crops followed by seven years of famine. He then convinces the Pharaoh to act, and as the fourteen years come to be, Joseph becomes the second most powerful man in Egypt. I wanted to be like Joseph, able to see around corners and having the conviction and fortitude to play the long game. Public company CEOs need to communicate value-creation realities in their business and work to attract investors who buy in for that ride. In the end, you can't build long-term value for short-term investors or traders.

→ Private Capital Pools: Seeking Shared Goals

Similarly, private capital pools like the one I worked for while running Sims Sports can also be hard to discern as they will be driven by the unique objectives, goals, experiences, and styles of the individuals involved. It was as if these angel investors bought a lottery ticket and expected to will the business toward a wonderful outcome. Many angels lack investment sophistication and experience. No harm done when they are passive money. But when and if they are active, the challenges can be real.

Sims Sports was my first experience in a stand-alone company. I had four owners represented on the board. Two of them had additional investors behind them. The board members had big personalities. Often they used board time to redress investment terms between them that they felt were unfair. No single ownership group had control, and they were not aligned on how to build the company. For me, that became an unsolvable puzzle. As CEO it was difficult to keep their attention long enough to agree on a long-term plan for the business. My team needed to be designing and building product three seasons into the future to remain competitive. Operating in a highly competitive category with a dysfunctional and conflicted board and shareholder group is a tough hand to play.

→ Captured Companies: Negotiating Support for Your Plan

At Coleman, Russell Athletic, and later Fruit of the Loom, I was CEO of a captured company that had been acquired by a larger multi-business corporation. The approach I developed was to treat my bosses as if they were investors in my company. I took full responsibility for the company's vision, opportunity, strategy, and culture. Then I made it my responsibility to gain my bosses' support and trust for the plan. In my first year with Brooks as a captured business within Fruit of the Loom, we went to Bowling Green, Kentucky, for our budget review and presented our strategy and annual plan.

My boss was renowned for going line by line through every budget item. We were prepared for a long day. He leaned in with his pen on our budget, and it seemed like we would be starting the discussion by looking for places to cut excess from marketing, travel, and other nonessential initiatives. But just as we were to begin, he set down his pen. I was proud of the planning processes we had used (lifted from my days at Pillsbury). We may have been a smaller business within Fruit of the Loom, but we ran it with rigor, discipline, data, and analysis. We knew and owned our numbers. We were professional. We deserved to be trusted and empowered with autonomy—and we were.

→ Private Equity: A Mandate to Get a Return

Private equity brings to an operating business institutional capital managed by professional investors. Often, each firm has different investment theses and approaches to creating or realizing value. When I joined Brooks in 2001, it was a struggling company that had been acquired two years earlier by the private equity firm J.H. Whitney & Company. I had come to know the partners when I pitched them to invest in Sims Sports. Whitney didn't invest in Sims but later invited me to join the board of Brooks and ultimately to lead the company as CEO. In Brooks's darkest hour, Whitney stepped up to reinvest and gave us all the opportunity to turn the company around.

Since then, I've gotten quite a few calls from other entrepreneurs beginning to seek investment from private equity or venture capital. When they ask for my advice, I share my story and tell them they must do their homework and get to know the firm thoroughly. What are their goals? What is their time horizon? Are they at the beginning of a fund or at the end? Is the current fund in the money or in trouble? All of that is critical to understand how much time you may have to turn things around, build your business, and deliver value. If the fund you will be in is underwater with multiple failures, how much pressure might there be for your deal to become a sudden win? How do these investors operate with management teams? Are they going to roll up their sleeves and get involved in your business, or will they let you do your own thing? Are there relevant people to your business on the board or is it only the fund's partners? How much flexibility, runway, support, and patience will you have? Each fund is unique. Do not assume these investors will be your friends; they are your controlling financial partners. They are on a mission to get a return, and it is up to you to understand what that means for your business.

As Warren and Charlie say, you get the shareholders you deserve. In my experience, you also can and should earn your independence.

→ An Invitation to Omaha

Berkshire's Fruit of the Loom announced the acquisition of Russell Athletic, which included our Brooks Running, on April 17, 2006, appropriately the same day as the 110th running of the Boston Marathon. The months leading up to my providential conversation with Warren in January 2012 proved consequential. In the spring of 2011, he emailed to congratulate Brooks on its showing at the Berkshire annual meeting where we had the chance to showcase our brand, sell some product, and meet shareholders who love to talk to the people who run businesses that Warren and Charlie buy. We made a limited-edition "Berkshire Hathaway Shoe."

In the email, Warren admitted to receiving a pair of New Balance shoes some fifteen years earlier that he was still wearing ("I'm that kind of guy"). He let me know that his dress shoe size was 10.5 D in case I wanted to send him a replacement. After all, it could be embarrassing if he ever cracked three hours in a marathon and they took a photo. He also acknowledged needing two rest stops for a 100-yard dash.

I immediately sent him a care package of Brooks shoes and apparel, which he graciously acknowledged with a promise to retire his old New Balances. But it was his closing line that caught my attention. "If you are ever traveling east and have time to stop in Omaha for a steak, it would be great to see you." That invite was unexpected as I was still several levels below Berkshire—part of Russell, which reported to Fruit.

Not being shy, I found myself traveling east that summer. I walked into Berkshire's modest headquarters, which famously only had twenty-five employees (give or take) leading a sprawling

$110 billion company with more than 270,000 employees. I was ushered into Warren's office and began a three-hour meeting that was uninterrupted and without distractions from cell phones, calls, or urgent incoming issues. The door closes and you have Warren's undivided attention. It's like he has all the time in the world for you. He was warm, generous, curious, and enthusiastic. He brought a real passion for business to our conversation about the Brooks story. "How are you growing? How do you compete with Nike? Why don't they just squash you like a bug?"

Good questions, since Nike was sixty-eight times larger than Brooks that year.

My goal for the meeting was for Warren to fall in love with Brooks and the opportunity we had to build a unique and defendable brand in a great category with high returns on capital. I was in full pitch mode and talked at a hundred miles an hour. I talked about Brooks's journey away from the broad, everything-for-everyone athletic footwear and apparel business, and its rise as a company that focused on nothing but premium products for runners. I detailed how Brooks's intense product focus, distribution discipline, unparalleled customer service, and Run Happy essence set it apart from any other brand in the business. I highlighted Brooks's market share gains and growth, with sales increasing almost fourfold in the past decade. I knew he would appreciate Brooks's profitability and high returns on capital, a metric that made investment in growth a value-creation activity. The meeting moved fast as Warren asked questions that went from the customer dynamic to the supply chain.

Warren drove me to lunch to continue the conversation, and to make good on his offer of a steak, though we both chose salads instead. We talked about opportunities in China, changing consumer buying behavior, and the improving economy. I told him that he had been mentoring me from afar since the mid-1980s as I had read everything he wrote.

I flew home feeling fortunate. Tom Ross, our longtime head of finance and a key architect of the Brooks strategy, told me that lunch I had just enjoyed was worth a few million dollars. Warren annually auctions a lunch date—a one-on-one meal and conversation with him—to benefit GLIDE, a San Francisco–based social justice charity. In 2019 it sold to the highest bidder for $4.6 million.

As the holidays approached, Warren emailed again about a story he'd read in the *Wall Street Journal.* Facebook's Mark Zuckerberg had become a Brooks customer with his new Adrenaline GTS shoes, and Warren wanted me to know. "Keep pouring it on in 2012, we only need a few million more like Mark!" he concluded.

→ Brooks's Fourth Owner in Ten Years: Berkshire Hathaway

A few weeks later, Brooks became a stand-alone subsidiary of Berkshire Hathaway, and I sent Warren our 2011 annual report. It was a record year: 33 percent growth in revenue driving 43 percent growth in operating profit. Following the defining moments of the Great Recession and the barefoot earthquake, we'd seen our biggest product launch in history with the Pure-Project. Warren, who often handwrites short notes featuring an old drawing of himself (*Not a Recent Likeness), sent me a few encouraging words:

You are making me look good—not an easy job. Keep it up.

That October, Warren asked me to present Brooks's story and strategy to the Berkshire Hathaway Board of Directors. Given our small size within Berkshire, I was honored to be invited. Longtime Berkshire businesses like GEICO, BNSF Railway, Berkshire Hathaway Energy, and many others were all much larger companies. Brooks was also in only its first year as a direct subsidiary. Warren assured me that the directors would love to hear from me, and I was looking forward to the opportunity.

Given a firm sixty minutes, I walked them through our history, market, brand positioning, strategies, culture, and financial metrics. As Warren's question about Nike the previous year indicated, they wanted to know how we competed. I explained that Brooks stands for performance product excellence as it is the first step in creating brand engagement and trust. Runners will serve as the ultimate judges of our success. They'll vote with their feet and their dollars.

Figure 8

To illustrate what we consider to be our unique brand recipe, I projected a slide showing three major ingredients: biomechanics & science, art, and runner insights. This mixture is seasoned with a healthy sprinkling of Run Happy (see figure 8).

We effectively compete against dozens of brands many times our size because we are driven to build the best running gear in the world, plus we excel at engaging and connecting with runners and serving the market as a niche expert.

Figure 9 shows how I see the overlap with Brooks and Berkshire Hathaway:

BROOKS AND BERKSHIRE OVERLAP

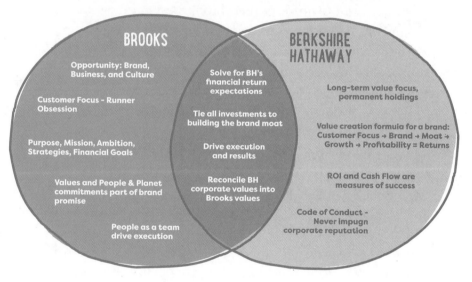

Figure 9

At every annual meeting in May, you will see Berkshire employees, shareholders, and visitors running along the Missouri River waterfront in Omaha on Sunday morning, and many were asking us to put on a 5K race. Warren picked up on the idea, and we created the Berkshire Hathaway "Invest in Yourself" 5K in 2013.

Warren announced an invitation to shareholders that the first "Berkshire 5K Race" would be run on Sunday morning after the meeting. "Regretfully, I will forego running: Someone has to man the starting gun." The race has become an annual affair. Each year, Buffett and Munger announce the race at the outset of the meeting. Although everyone should sign up, the two leaders plan to sleep in. But they do wish everyone a good run.

→ Corporate Governance at Berkshire

Berkshire Hathaway has a unique business model among Fortune 100 companies. Its twenty-five or so headquarters' employees morph to the needs of their businesses, not the other way around. As the new guy wanting to get our company's owner all the information it would need to understand and track our business, I asked Warren and his noninsurance vice chair, Greg Abel, what information and reports they wanted to receive on Brooks.

Warren responded: Send along the front page of the summary income statement and whatever else you look at that you think is important. The only required meeting was to set my compensation each year. He directed me to handle the compensation for everyone else at Brooks. No need to send expense reports to Berkshire; your controller can approve them. He told me we could issue our own press release about the move to Berkshire. "Your judgment on the wording will also be fine." Charlie Munger has often spoken about a "seamless web of deserved trust" as a life pursuit, and Berkshire's culture reflects that philosophy. As a manager within the company, I can confirm that having trust weighs heavy. Having been given complete trust, I am highly focused on delivering on every level as I alone own all the outcomes.

I made it a point to travel to Omaha once a year to meet Warren and review Brooks's strategy and progress. The culture I experience is encouragement and support. Warren invests in people and lets them run. In our early conversations, I had asked Warren if he would be open to us creating a board of advisors at Brooks. Although I didn't know her personally yet, I suggested that Charlotte Guyman, who lives in the Seattle area and serves on the Berkshire board, would be a terrific member. He supported the idea enthusiastically, and today Greg Abel at Berkshire is recommending the approach to other Berkshire companies.

My goals were to recreate what we'd had at Whitney: a super smart board of diverse experiences with whom our senior leadership team could engage to make us better. I had missed the sounding board but also knew our leadership team would benefit by having to prepare strategies and plans for people who would challenge us and ask lots of questions. We had gotten to the point of almost being able to finish each other's sentences. I took a page from a CEO friend who had a very effective advisory board model for his private company and created the following board concept for Brooks:

- **Goal:** Tackle and grapple with important questions; avoid time-consuming and un-fun fiduciary committee and regulatory duties! Selfishly, the meetings were more about the needs of the leadership team than those of the board. It was about learning, scaling, tuning our plans, and benefiting from the board's experiences to guide us.
- **Format:** Non-Fiduciary Advisory Board, four meetings per year limited to a short seven-hour day from 8:00 a.m. to 3:00 p.m., with working lunch.
- **Meeting Focus:** Business review with deep dives into select strategic questions with the goal of having the board members do at least 40 percent of the talking. We would also extend an invite to Brooks events to experience our brand and culture.

Now in place for nearly a decade, our Brooks Advisory Board has had a huge impact on our team and company. Punching above our weight class, we have attracted incredible talent, including people like Robbie Bach, former Microsoft president of entertainment and devices (Xbox); Deanna Oppenheimer, former vice chair of Barclays Bank; Charlotte Guyman, Berkshire Hathaway board member and former Microsoft executive; Anne Rohosy, former Nike executive and president of Levi Strauss Americas; Darrell Cavens, cofounder of Zulily; and Robin Thurston, CEO of Outside, Inc., founder of MapMyFitness, and former chief digital officer of Under Armour.

With our advisory board, we now had the best of both worlds: the trust and accountability granted by Berkshire, and a top-notch group of people to sharpen our thinking and mentor us as we navigated challenges and opportunities.

→ Warren Buffett at Brooks

That generous spirit was on full display when Warren joined our entire global team for a town hall meeting in Seattle, marking our hundredth anniversary as a brand. The event, staged in Seattle's historic Moore Theatre, was moderated by Charlotte Guyman. Charlotte began by asking Warren what everyone in the room wanted to hear: Why did he spin Brooks out of Fruit of the Loom and make it a direct report?

In his signature Nebraska frankness, he said, "Brooks was too good a company and had too much going for it to be a subsidiary of Fruit. No offense to Fruit, but I spotted what [Brooks] was doing and it just deserved to be a direct subsidiary. And besides, when anything is going to be successful as Brooks, I want to take credit for it, frankly!"

He moved on to his other business framework: the importance of a business to build its moat. "If you have an economic castle—and Brooks has a castle—someone is going to try to take it away from you." He said two things are needed: "First, you need the right knight guarding the place, and we've got the right knight." He briefly glanced at me, and I was momentarily taken aback by the spotlight as the Brooks team erupted in applause. "Then you need a moat around the castle," he continued. "And you need to keep throwing piranha and sharks and snakes in there, because people are going to try to cross it.

"The ultimate moat is a great brand, but protecting that moat requires getting that brand into the head of every runner or potential runner in the world, having them have an expectation about that brand, and then meeting that expectation. And if you do that, the moat keeps widening. People are always going to want to run. And they're going to have something in their mind about all of the better-known brands. And what you want in their mind about Brooks is that it's going to bring out the best in them and do the most for them, and then you can't disappoint them. And if you do that, the sky is the limit.

"Running will always be with us. More and more people around the world will run more and more. The demand will never disappear. You've got to encourage that demand and adapt to it in certain ways. But [running] is something that's so fundamental that we don't need to worry about the business going away."

He concluded: "Brooks is doing what it absolutely should be doing. You are improving the lives of people who use your product, and we haven't scratched the surface yet."

→ Lessons Learned at Berkshire

Over the past decade, many of us at Brooks, especially me, have accumulated invaluable lessons from Warren. And we're still learning. Entire books and business review articles have been dedicated to the Oracle of Omaha. And rightly so. I'm often asked what it's like to work with Berkshire Hathaway and its leaders. I've never enjoyed greater autonomy in my business career, and I've never felt so accountable and responsible. Of all the ownership structures I have experienced, it is the closest to owning the business and being entirely responsible for it. Why? Complete autonomy with complete accountability.

Warren seeks people with passion, and he does his homework. Attract and retain people with a lot of passion for their business. You want people who are in love with their business. Warren told our team at Brooks that he imagines himself as Michelangelo going to the Sistine Chapel every morning. He could do anything else, but he wants to be there in that office working on his masterpiece.

There are a lot of values and attributes I experience in working with Berkshire. Among those I most admire are:

Integrity

Warren tells executives to look for three qualities in the people they hire: intelligence, energy, and integrity. He adds if you don't have the last one, don't even bother with the first two. Charlie Munger has his ABCs—avoiding arrogance, bureaucracy, and complacency. We remind ourselves of them often. Warren also taught me that a CEO is the chief risk officer. Risk is not something to be delegated. To that, he appends the quip not to do anything you wouldn't want to see on the front page of the daily newspaper. A chief risk officer's responsibilities include hiring high integrity people who take accountability seriously. Charlie and Warren believe in a culture in which trust is earned. It is deserved or not deserved. A company like Enron had great vision and values statements and books of rules and policies, but they weren't worth the paper they were printed on, because so many people from the top down ignored them and behaved badly.

Empowered Culture

There is one Berkshire meeting for managers each year and the lineup includes a luncheon and CEO panels on relevant business topics. I first attended in 2013. Warren hosted the lunch, a simple affair with burgers on one side and salads on the other. No slides or spreadsheets. He just stood up and spent a few minutes highlighting a good year across the businesses and thanked everyone for their efforts. He said the only failure was on him because he couldn't find an acquisition that year to invest the cash flow all of the businesses were creating. "Let's have a good year next year too." And that was it. The only business meeting of the year for one of the most significant companies in America had lasted about ten minutes.

Stay in Your Circle of Competence

At one of the annual meetings, he saw the managers of his three furniture companies standing together in a hallway. "I hope you aren't talking about synergies, because I bought three great companies. I don't want them to become one." He lets each business do its thing. It's not a team. It's a portfolio of aggressively run businesses, and it works. This intense focus on discrete customers and markets fits Brooks's DNA perfectly.

Praise

Warren and Charlie offer glowing feedback for their roughly sixty Berkshire managers and CEOs. In meetings, each of their faces are projected, and he thanks them sincerely. If you are ever mentioned in his annual letter, it is a feather in your cap for value-added performance. Warren believes in praising publicly and criticizing privately.

Permanence

In his letters and his original 1996 "Owner's Manual," Warren discusses the gift of a permanent home with financial strength to the companies they acquire. There is no gin rummy managerial behavior (discard your least promising business at each turn) at Berkshire. The days of dealing with banks and Wall Street analysts are forever ended. Berkshire is a unique acquirer for a closely held or family-owned business that wants to stay involved.

Society

Warren doesn't miss an opportunity to remind everyone how much we should appreciate America and its opportunities as an engine for improving people's lives with the rule of law, capitalism, and democracy. "There has been no incubator for unleashing human potential like America," Buffett said in his 2020 message to shareholders. Even though progress can be slow, uneven, and discouraging at times, never bet against America.

I've learned a lot from Warren and Charlie's generation, often referred to as "the Greatest Generation" for good reasons. More recently, America's largest generation, millennials, taught us a new set of lessons.

CHAPTER 7

Pivot #2: Performance Is Timeless (We Zig When They Zag)

R UNNING WAS ENTERING ITS THIRD DECADE of growth. The original running boom sparked by Frank Shorter's gold medal performance in the 1972 Olympic marathon resumed in the late 1990s with a second boom. Running had remained one of the largest, most inclusive sports and fitness activities in the world. We estimated there were more than 130 million people running worldwide with nearly forty million in the United States alone.

→ Millennials Bust the Running Boom

The millennial generation (born between 1981 and 1996, according to the Pew Research Center), was key to growth as they were by far the largest demographic in running. For that reason, they were always in our sights. Brooks is present with high school and college runners who are involved in the sport from cross country to track and field. However, the large athletic brands are better known. Our strategy was to introduce ourselves to new runners as they hit their mid-twenties and began to invest in their physical fitness. Once they start to work and begin to form households, they tend to make choices about how to stay active. Running often makes the cut.

Brooks came out of 2014 intensely focused on self-defined runners (SDRs) over the age of twenty-five, which represented about half of the millennial generation with more joining the twenty-five-plus segment focus every year. Typically, this person is interested in performance gear, willing to pay more for it, and often quite influential to casual runners. To grow as a performance running brand, we needed them to choose us. We also believed that when it came to marketing our products and brand, age groups were not that relevant or actionable. In our research, the reasons people ran and how it made them feel seemed to transcend age. If we concentrated on reasons why people ran and all the behaviors around how it fit into their lives, we would position ourselves to win with them whatever their age.

As it turned out, this assumption on runner behavior was a huge mistake. While their running habits may look similar, in fact nearly everything else about millennials made them dramatically different than any previous demographic group.

Numbering approximately 72.1 million, the millennial generation (also called Generation Y) is the largest age group in US history. Therefore, where they go, so goes the market. They are digital natives, born or at least raised online and socially connected. They have less money to spend, more debt, and different priorities than their parents' generation. According to the Pew Research Center, they put off commitments like marriage and home ownership. Goldman Sachs research shows millennials prefer a "sharing economy" that provides access to products such as cars and luxury goods, without needing to own them.

In our business, if you get old with your customer, you end up getting left behind. We were building a brand to stand the test of time, which meant we also needed to attract young adults. Are they going to know Brooks, and will we be part of their journey?

→ Consumer Focus: "Go to Where the Puck Is Going"

I'm a big fan of this phrase by Wayne Gretzky's father, Walter Gretzky, as it is relevant for any consumer brand. Especially in times of rapid change, you must sense where the action will be, not where the puck has been. I think it is one of the hardest skill sets to build in business. There were many questions on what the Generation Y runner really wanted. After the Great Recession, there was a new frugality. Financial pressures began to build on household income. Education, housing, and healthcare costs escalated much faster than wages. With discretionary dollars dear, what products would make the cut?

Fitness and exercise were fragmenting into many new opportunities from yoga to fitness studios like Orange Theory and CrossFit, and free fitness experiences like November Project and Parkrun in Europe. Millennials were seemingly less serious or competitive in any one sport. They were dabbling in many, moving from one activity to another. It seemed they were less interested in expensive technical gear, which they saw as just filling up their apartment or garage. Instead, they were buying less expensive alternatives and even renting when possible. The new "sharing" economy was creating questions and uncertainty in every category.

Participation in running races began to fall. We hit a wall. On May 5, 2016, a *Wall Street Journal* article with the headline

"How Millennials Ended the Running Boom" got everyone's attention. The conventional wisdom was building that not only was the running boom over, but there were also many other activities to capture the time and energy of millennials and deliver the experiences they appeared to desire. The outlook for running was clouded.

Many argued that the drop in participation was because millennials were more into screens and virtual reality experiences. But what we saw was that this group was actually more active than any generation before. They simply didn't want to self-identify with a single activity. They were hungry to try it all.

At Brooks, we had many debates to assess where millennials would end up. Where would running fit into their lives? How did organized runs and races fit into their new eclectic fitness lifestyle? What types of products would address what they needed and wanted? Would it be cheaper, simpler, tech-light offerings that every brand in athletic, outdoor, fitness, and now increasingly many of the fashion brands were aggressively delivering? This was not a pretty picture for Brooks. That was not our strength. It was yet another major product trend like the barefoot-inspired, minimalist shoe boom that did not favor Brooks. Were millennials all going to want cheap, wannabe, athleisure products? That prospect was extremely unsettling as trepidation returned for us at Brooks.

As we began to project how products would evolve to meet millennials' running needs, we also had to come to grips with the new frugality in the market. Many millennials had significant debt hangovers from college. They had watched their parents go through the Great Recession—some losing their homes and most losing equity in the homes they kept. It wasn't clear that performance running gear at premium prices would make the cut with them. Did millennials even want a performance technical product? Would they be willing to pay $120 to $160 for a performance running shoe, $50 for a running bra, $100 for a running jacket? Clearly, many seemed willing to spend more on experiences and less on products.

Nike could afford to put chips on every color and number on the table. We couldn't. Conventional wisdom said we needed to merchandize to where the market went. We said no. To be true to our brand, we went fishing in different waters, away from the crowd, to where we thought the market was going.

Another challenger brand, Under Armour, was reaching for gold against its competitors. Under Armour had been on fire in the last decade and was nipping at Nike's business. Its founder, Kevin Plank, said on Bloomberg TV's *In the Loop* in 2015 that Adidas was his dumbest competitor. He wanted to go head-to-head with Nike. He saw his brand and culture as that of a competitor on a field of play. Us against them. But for brands, it's not like that. The customer is in charge. The customer pays the bill. You either solve for the customer or you don't. A few years later, Adidas pulled ahead of Under Armour, whose sales had sagged. Plank announced he would step down as CEO of the company he founded.

→ Where to Play: Performance Is Timeless, Right?

During this time, I began to lean on a quote often attributed to Thomas Jefferson that seemed to define our task in these confusing times: *In matters of style, swim with the current; in matters of principle, stand like a rock.* By 2016 things were becoming clearer to us. While lower-priced, basic product was selling broadly from other brands, it was also evident that the decline in performance running shoes and apparel was partly due to boring product. Brands looked more the same than different. There was simply nothing exciting or distinctive as you looked across the walls, racks, or websites selling performance running gear. Having let our line get stale, we now looked too much like the competitors.

Had we taken our eye off where the puck was going? Maybe. Since the barefoot craze, we had some of our best people at Brooks focused on the clinical research in and around our Run Signature initiatives. Our clinical studies with hundreds of runners had led us to key insights about the uniqueness of habitual joint motion from runner to runner. Our learnings in this research were shared in white papers and would be critically important for future innovation across our product line.

At the same time, rising costs led us to create our first footwear manufacturing base outside of China in Vietnam. While this was something we had to do, it distracted the team from creating much needed innovation and quality.

It was time, once again, for Brooks to zig when the entire industry was zagging. We believed a millennial-led market would respond to innovation that delivered on a better experience. Our team would once again dig deep and deliver.

Patrick Pons de Vier, a rugby-playing Frenchman from the Alps, arrived at Brooks at just the right moment. Or, as he would tell it, he arrived like a black cat. Everything was about to go south. It was March 2015, and he joined us to lead global footwear after a highly successful, twenty-year career at Salomon and Amer Sports, owner of ski brands like Atomic, Arc'teryx, and Salomon boots. In addition to his career credentials, Patrick also was a former punk-rock drummer who favored The Clash and the Sex Pistols. He had already been a key architect of building a $1 billion shoe business at Salomon, and we wanted to be his second billion-dollar brand.

He hit the ground running. A leader of strategy, people, and process, Patrick and team built a new ten-year vision that we called Runtopia. He drove detailed comprehensive initiatives to fully develop Brooks's now full menu of capabilities: Run Signature technologies; Run Sights lab research; a Brooks Academy to train the team on Brooks fit, quality, and craftmanship;

an aggressive innovation agenda; and a crafted beauty design aesthetic. All of this plus great margins.

At the time, our leadership team was actively debating which customers we were going after. Should we open our aperture from SDRs (self-defined runners) older than twenty-five to all who run, adding millions of occasional and casual runners to our focus? Retro, lifestyle shoes from the seventies and eighties were in fashion again, and we brought back our old Vantage design as part of the Brooks Heritage line to celebrate our hundredth anniversary. Should we invest to grow that, even though it's no longer a performance run product? Should we create take-down product and lower price points and go into family footwear and mid-price department store channels? Should we develop a line for the casual, lifestyle customer that the athleisure and big brands were all rushing to? Should we refresh the kids' shoe business and create a new line? Was it time to expand distribution as most every other major brand had done via Amazon and Kohl's? Did we even have the products and brand strength to do that?

Many of these paths were treacherous for a premium brand like Brooks. Our category was littered with brands that ended up losing focus on running's core customer: the frequent participant, self-defined runner over the age of twenty-five. In a quest to grow, many created new customers at lower price points and traded down others, losing their performance credibility with discerning runners.

In the end it was clear that to grow profitably, Brooks needed to win in performance and gain share with runners, even if there would be fewer of them. Regardless, we had to reinvent our products and commit to innovation and improved fit, feel, ride, and design. Patrick was galvanizing the team around innovation driven by runner insight and getting us out of our conservative, fixed box to innovate in design. In a few short years, there would be a renaissance of new footwear products, and apparel would follow.

→ Replanting Our Brooks Flag in Performance

I stood up for my keynote presentation at our global sales meeting in Seattle in May 2016. Hundreds of pairs of eyes looked at me, especially sales representatives who stood every day on the front lines with retailers who needed to ring the till. I knew it might not be what they wanted to hear, but I enthusiastically replanted Brooks's flag firmly in performance products for runners, declaring "Performance Is Timeless." We were not going to chase the athleisure trend. There would always be plenty of runners who wanted, needed, and even demanded the best, mile after mile. We would declare that every runner deserved performance. We again burned a few boats as we exited the heritage footwear business, the kids shoe business, and fitness-inspired, "performance light" apparel.

Figure 10

We revamped our entire Brooks product line with runner-focused innovation and attention to detail in trainers, race day shoes, run bras, foul weather and visibility solutions, and go-everywhere gear including trail. Brooks was back, but it was a lonely path (see figure 10). We were one of the only major brands that was investing heavily in performance technology. The other was Nike, which played in every segment of the industry. It was innovating in uppers with Flyknit and would soon launch its spring-loaded Alphafly NEXT% technology. Time would tell which brands would be in the right place to pick up the puck, shoot, and score.

→ Digital Shopping Takes Center Stage

Brooks's sweet spot in marketing campaigns has always been connecting our brand with every runner wherever they are on their running journey, whether competing for a spot on the Olympic team, having just hit the standard for the trials, or completing their first 5K. In June 2017, we hit the bull's-eye in our efforts to celebrate everyone's run with a novel approach we called the Big Endorsement Campaign.

While many runners dream of becoming professional athletes, big-time endorsement deals in running are generally reserved for the fastest in the world. We decided to change that. On Global Running Day, June 7, 2017, Brooks announced the largest sports endorsement deal in history. Any runner who wanted to become an endorsed Brooks athlete would receive a check for $1 and access to special content on training and nutrition. We thought maybe twenty thousand runners would take advantage of these bragging rights. More than eighty thousand took us up on the offer.

We needed more than one creative campaign to reach millennials. They didn't just make waves in the sport with how they ran and in what gear; their shopping behavior was changing fast and disrupting both brand and retailers. Some ten years after the introduction of the iPhone, consumers were decidedly in charge.

Our research confirmed that approximately 30 percent of runners bought their shoes online in 2017. In a few short years, Amazon.com had captured a 10 percent market share, becoming the number one running-shoe retailer. Also, more than 60 percent of online searches for running shoes now started on Amazon versus Google or Bing. In-store traffic was down across retail channels, but average ticket and conversions were up, confirming that consumers often researched online and via smartphones before visiting a store. Runners were now often starting their shopping journey online and then buying everywhere.

We continued to believe the brick-and-mortar experience would have a place in the future, but trends now reflected a barbell market with price and convenience on one end (such as Amazon, Zappos, BrooksRunning.com, FleetFeet.com, DicksSportingGoods.com, and REI.com) and an engaging in-store shopping experience on the other. These stores offered a combination of service, community, local relevance, expertise, curation, gait analysis, running groups, training advice, and race registration. The retailers in the middle, often typified by big-box, low-service sporting goods like the Sports Authority, were in trouble. We saw more than nine hundred stores shutter in 2016 alone, including 463 at the Sports Authority.

Amazon was important, but it was not the answer for a brand like Brooks. They were not a premium-brand–friendly partner. It was a constant battle to manage our brand presentation, as their algorithms drove internet prices to the bottom. They were a harvester of demand, not a servicer to help runners find the right shoe and fit. Nor were they a storyteller of products and technology. We ultimately decided not to sell Amazon inventory as they had no ability to position technical product. Instead, we chose to be on Amazon Marketplace only, where we could control presentation and merchandising mix. Amazon

then unceremoniously kicked us off! Not exactly an open platform for sellers to connect with customers. Amazon decided it
wanted everything or you were out.

We got creative by picking our best retail partners and having them represent Brooks in Amazon Marketplace. Today,
runners are there, and they are finding Brooks available from
many of our best retail partners.

Before the dust settled on all the turmoil at retail, we made
two critical, foundational judgments at Brooks:

1. We had to aggressively invest in *digital marketing* to
    engage with runners as they were shopping online.
    The first shoe shelf a runner now sees is not in a
    physical store but online. If we were not present
    when and where they shopped, it would be as if we
    did not exist.
2. We reaffirmed our commitment to win with the best
    Specialty Run and Sporting Goods Retailers in
    running. We believed many would survive with their
    strong service, community runner connection, and
    their own growing digital businesses. Just as Walmart
    had failed to put all retailers out of business in the
    nineties, we believed Amazon would not destroy
    every retailer. The strong would adapt and survive.
    We wanted to be their lead vendor in run.

A key step in addressing runners' evolving shopping behavior
was hiring Melanie Allen as Brooks's first true chief marketing
officer. Melanie was an accomplished marketer with some twenty
years of experience at Starbucks and P&G. She would lead the
team to create programs to generate demand across digital pipes
but with an agnostic view of where they purchased our gear.
Brooks had the strongest retail distribution of any brand in the
running category, and we wanted to drive demand not only to

our own website, but to wherever a runner wanted to buy and Brooks was sold. Melanie and Dan Sheridan, who was then general manager and head of Brooks's global sales, collaborated to create cross-functional programs, metrics, and digital connections to feed demand and guide runners to where they could purchase Brooks gear. We ran the numbers. After direct costs, our contribution margin from our wholesale business was essentially equal to the profit on our direct-to-consumer, e-commerce business. We decided to squelch the internal competition between wholesale and direct and put everyone on the same goals: Create digital demand with runners and harvest wherever they wanted to shop as efficiently and with the least friction possible. We prioritized investments in tools that would create an omnichannel consumer experience in a multichannel world.

→ **Maintaining Culture in Challenging Times**

It has been said that when times get tough, people's true values are revealed. The same can be said for companies. In difficult moments when you have to make choices, pick a path, select which investments you must make, and jettison all the others. You must differentiate the nice-to-haves from the must-haves. The extremely challenging times in 2015–2016 would force us to make choices at Brooks, and in the end these decisions exposed what we believed, stood for, and valued as a brand.

I love these moments. They are competitive strategy gold for a niche challenger brand, because they are market signaling opportunities with a megaphone. We would step out in the open and declare our convictions, and the world (or at least the industry) would listen and pass judgment as to whether we were visionary or crazy.

Of course, there's always been a culture at Brooks. There was one before I arrived (several industry folks counseled me to not mess it up). In my early days, I may have taken Brooks's culture for granted. But because culture is in essence a collection of behaviors by a group of people, it is never static. It can morph for better or worse over time, even overnight, especially for a company in growth mode. In 2014, we began in earnest to work on leading and scaling Brooks's culture. Our recent growth meant we had added a lot of new people. There were many questions across the team about what exactly the Brooks culture was. We had spent a great deal of time defining what our brand stood for in running and that was well codified across the organization. But we were in the early stages of formally articulating to team members what our values were and what they looked like in our leaders. I regularly presented the slide in figure 11 to illustrate Brooks's signature approach of building great gear plus connecting with runners (with a refreshing twist of authenticity!). The truth was I would often think of Brooks's culture the same way: Serious about our gear but not taking ourselves too seriously. Work hard, play hard.

Brooks Signature Cocktail

Authentic Storytelling

Emotional Engagement

Great Gear

Figure 11

A few years earlier, we began capturing net promoter scores (NPS) with customers to measure brand affinity. NPS is calculated by taking the percentage of customers rating their likelihood to recommend a company, a product, or a service to a friend or colleague as nine or ten ("Promoters") minus the percentage rating this at six or below ("Detractors") on a scale from zero to ten. Respondents who provide a score of seven or eight are referred to as "Passives" and do indeed enter into the overall percentage calculation.

We valued this analysis highly. Our NPS score was always at or near the top relative to our competition. For a performance brand, affinity with core customers is currency. For a challenger brand like Brooks, the success formula includes creating zealots and brand love with your target customers. NPS measured that, too. Hence, we thought if it worked for customers, why not our employees?

In March 2015, we presented to our board of advisors the results of our first real employee survey intended to measure our cultural health at Brooks. We had a highly connected and collaborative spirit and work-hard ethic followed by celebrating success. These elements had always been part of Brooks's culture. It mirrored the experience of a good hard run followed by high fives and a beer with friends. Yet as we grew, siloes developed. We knew that championing values including trust, thought leadership, innovation, and playing as a team were opportunities across the company, and the survey results confirmed it.

When times got tough in 2016, our employee NPS dropped. In one sense, it was logical. Things were uncertain at Brooks, so your likelihood of recommending the company to a friend would be lower. This bothered me because what mattered over the long haul was how we behaved against our shared values day in and day out, especially when facing headwinds. Ironically, I thought it was clear we were making progress on living our values and the leadership team was more engaged on the topic than ever before. We were working on building trust, pursuing innovation, playing as a team, celebrating wins, solving problems, and helping one another out. And yet, our employee NPS said we were getting weaker?

→ Measuring Cultural Strength: Values in Action

Enter Katie Carlson, who had recently been promoted to run the global human resources team and joined our executive committee. In solving for culture, Katie and her team had a key insight. Employee NPS did not measure the strength of our values in action; it was actually just an employee happiness score. What mattered was how we were behaving against our stated values, whether we had a tailwind of growth or a headwind of challenges. This led to a complete revamp of our culture survey to measure behaviors against our values. The survey data would allow us to challenge ourselves as leaders to get better at leading culture in both good and challenging times.

This insight would inspire the creation of Brooks's "Connect" Leadership Development Training program for people managers of all levels and tenures across the global team. Katie led her team to architect the Connect program that would graduate more than 130 managers from its five-day curriculum in its first cohort. The program challenges everyone to use both heart and mind as we lead our people to scale Brooks's collaborative, connected culture against our stated values and behaviors (see figure 12).

The adage of never letting a good crisis go to waste has truth in it, but can sometimes seem trite. After all, building culture is hard work and it's never done. There is no doubt we strengthened our brand, our company, and our culture coming out of the reinvention of performance running in 2016, but we had to work hard for it. Our cultural strengths survey results have

BROOKS BRAND VALUES

RUNNER FIRST.

At the center of everything we do is the runner — our obsession, our inspiration, our path forward. When in doubt, solve for the runner.

- Lead with runners by acting on insights with the courage and conviction to push past the expected.
- Stay curious and get to know the runner.
- Balance facts and sound judgment to take smart, informed risks.
- Challenge assumptions and test new ideas and opportunities that have impact and potential.
- Be brave enough to fail. Learn from it, and move on.

WORD IS BOND.

Authentic brands are built on trust. Do what you say you will.

- Embody the kind of integrity that turns acquaintances into advocates.
- Our brand and products are implicit promises to customers — keep your promises.
- Treat every human being with dignity and respect.
- Communicate with clarity and transparency, keep it real, keep it simple, be accountable.
- Share information with teammates openly and proactively.
- Emphasize inclusivity and equality in pursuit of a more just world.

CHAMPION HEART.

We are in this game to win. Take nothing for granted. Give it your all.

- Customers have choices. Make it easy to choose Brooks.
- Protect our moat. The competition wants what we have.
- Come to the line believing we can win.
- Pursue a level of excellence that gives you deep pride.
- Set aggressive goals and high standards that surprise and delight the customer and deliver results for the brand and business.
- Practice and progress to avoid the "I've arrived" mentality that leads to innovation atrophy.

THERE'S NO "I" IN RUN.

None of us can do alone what all of us can do together. Be generous with your humanity.

- Seek to make contributions instead of taking credit.
- Support and engage in processes that drive action and align all team members for growth and success.
- Make connections with all who run, our customers, partners, communities, and each other.
- Develop a strong sense of self and situational awareness and then lean into that knowledge to engage with people.
- Listen openly, communicate clearly, give and receive feedback, and manage with mind and heart.
- Seek diverse perspectives, viewpoints, styles, and identities; actively listen to opposing points of view.
- Accept that sometimes you will need to support decisions with which you disagree.
- Give something unexpected that adds value to your teammates, our partners, and the community.

KEEP MOVING.

Run. Or find a way to move every day. Joy is kinetic.

- Stay active. Momentum is a powerful force, both for your health and your career.
- We want you here — take care of yourself so you can bring your best self every day.
- Exercise optimism in a way that improves the day for those around you.
- Broaden your world by learning about others' experiences.
- When you're stuck, ask for help.
- Celebrate successes and plan the next ones.
- Life's short — enjoy the journey.

Figure 12

improved every year since we put the focus on behaviors that reflect our values. Most telling, as we entered the fourth month of the COVID-19 work-from-home mode, our culture scores went up in 2020! The team came out stronger, and it was earned. Our voluntary turnover goal is to be less than 12 percent and 2020 would come in at 11.9 percent, in a roller-coaster year.

CHAPTER 8

Finding Another Gear While Navigating Global Disruptions

→ Charting Brooks's Future

By the third quarter of 2017, we were growing again. Patrick's leadership was making an impact, and our footwear team created our strongest collection in years with remarkable execution on core styles, fit, quality, and key new products like the Revel. The Revel was a fast, clean, bold design at the customer-friendly $100 price point that would be more approachable for new runners. We characterized the market of the time as a knockdown, drag-out, product war with dozens of brands and hundreds of products vying for runners' attention. For a product to break through, it had to look, fit, ride, and be great.

Brooks's ability to attract new runners was back. We had planted our flag firmly in performance and were communicating that at every turn. We were making progress on digital engagement and finally showing commitment and investment in partnering with the best retailers in run globally. It was a new and improved playbook, and it was beginning to work. We had found another gear for the brand and I used this graphic (figure 13) to share our momentum with the team:

Figure 13

As we were making progress on nurturing our culture, it was clear we needed stronger alignment and integration in our planning process to get everyone in sync, not just the leadership team. We were a small global brand in a big category. Our challenge was to go to market as a full synchronized team and bring our product and brand stories alive online, in thousands of retailers, and wherever runners ran. We wanted them to understand our technologies and sense the spirit of our brand, which celebrated their individual run. Runner to runner, human to human.

→ Creating a Playbook to Drive Integration and Alignment

We needed to align everyone globally on this more detailed road map and playbook. We called it "Charting Brooks's Future." This fourteen-page document defined our three-year plans and attempted to bring all of our initiatives together and force integration and alignment across everyone's plans. Updated annually, it would highlight key decisions and priorities; it would drive work plans to deliver on "all of the play-it-through lines" for our teams around the world. The challenge for this document was to communicate comprehensively and efficiently as Albert Einstein said, "Everything should be made as simple as possible, but no simpler."

The document included a concise articulation of Brooks's unique opportunity to build an authentic brand in run distinct from the large athletic brands. It set forth clear long-term goals including financial, customer, operational, and culture metrics. We then spelled out a framework for leading the plan, allocating resources, and setting priorities. Out of necessity, we created a clumsy acronym called FLO-EEA-T (pronounced "flow-eat"). This was our attempt to shorten the internal articulation of the three pillars capturing every aspect of Brooks's strategy: *Front Line Obsession, Extreme Enterprise Accountability, and Team.*

The acronym may be inelegant, but its impact was enormous. By having FLOEEAT frame every departmental initiative and budget item, we got the team focused on what mattered:

- **Front Line Obsession (Growth)**—Putting customers first as they are in charge
    Great Gear—Footwear, Run Bras, Apparel
    Runner at the Center—Connecting, Prospecting, Converting
    Market Execution—Wholesale, Direct, New Markets

- **Extreme Enterprise Accountability (Profitability)**— Running the business profitably to accelerate brand momentum and create a flywheel
    Gross Margin Management
    Inventory Optimization
    Business Model Efficiency
    Risk Management

- **T**eam (Culture and People)—Creating a sustained culture and team dynamic that attract talented people who can execute Brooks's strategy successfully, year in, year out
    Planet and People
    Connected Culture
    Inclusion and Appreciation

Next, we created a grid to hold decisions we made and set-tled for the team. They were prioritized and sequenced over the next three years, so there was no need to debate them. We stack ranked all our budget priorities, strategies, opportunities, and initiatives with the following framework:

- *Strategic Criticality*—Rank the necessity from a strategy and business point of view that we lead in this area to assure long- and/or short-term success.
    Win (W): Critical success factor—need leadership and team focus to assure success.
    Compete (C): Need to be competitive against industry standards in execution. Could be an initiative in a ramping mode.
    Play (P): On the strategic road map for our business and brand but recognize that we need to execute with defined resources until a future time.

- *Investment Priority*—We need to make sure resources are focused for success against specific areas of incremental impact.
    Invest (I): Incremental resources required above baseline to deliver on priorities.
    Maintain (M): Resources are held in line as a percent of sales (variable costs) or with inflation on headcount and overhead. Mix within function is optimized to priorities.
    Right Size/Divest (RS/D): This initiative or spending needs to be reduced so resources can be moved to critical priorities.

- *Sequencing Priority*—No business can do everything at once as financial resources, people, systems, and bandwidth will not allow. Sequencing investments and projects over the next three years to maximize impact and reduce risks is the goal.

This framework pulled a heavy oar in removing all of the win/lose mindsets across departments. All decisions, funding, and new headcount would be scored against the established criteria. It dramatically streamlined decision making and drove alignment and integration. Figure 14 is a sample of the grid that prioritized our customer focus.

It has been a key tool for new people coming into the team to learn and understand the playbook and connect it to the big picture on brand, business, and culture. FLOEEAT was here to stay.

→ Des Linden "Shows Up" to Win Boston

April 16, 2018, was an unforgettable day for Brooks and distance running fans in the United States. It marked the 122nd running of the Boston Marathon, widely regarded as the pinnacle annual marathon in the world given the prequalification standards runners must hit to participate. Brooks had a handful of strong, endorsed runners toeing the line. The two with the greatest potential to win were Americans Des Linden and Shadrack Biwott. This was big for us. Brooks did not have athletes on Olympic podiums.

Running a marathon, particularly at the elite level, involves calculated preparation with customized plans around training, nutrition, sleep, and more. Performance gear choices are critical, as one errant stitch or misplaced flex groove matters over 26.2 miles and can make the difference between the podium and a DNF (did not finish). Runners control all of these choices. But

CUSTOMER FOCUS

Strategic Criticality: Win **(W)** Compete **(C)** Play **(P)**
Investment Priority: Invest **(I)** Maintain **(M)** Right Size/Divest **(RS/D)**

	2018		2019		2020	
	Strategic Criticality	Investment Priority	Strategic Criticality	Investment Priority	Strategic Criticality	Investment Priority
RUN FREQUENCY / IDENTITY						
Self-Defined Runner (SDR) 1+ / week	W	I	W	I	W	I
Non-SDR 1+ / week	W	I	W	I	W	I
Non-runners	P	RS/D	P	RS/D	P	RS/D
MINDSETS						
Pacer, Soul Runner, Goal Seeker	W	I	W	I	W	I
High Fit Active	P	I	C	I	W	I
Solution Customer / Walker	P	M	C	M	C	M
Trail	P	M	P	M	P	M
PRICE						
Footwear > $100, Bras > $30	W	I	W	I	W	I
Footwear $75 - $100	P	M	P	M	P	M
Apparel > $30	P	M	P	M	P	M

Figure 14

as all long-distance runners know, despite perfect preparation, the one element you face on race day that you never control is weather. And that year the Boston Marathon packed a punch. Conditions were brutal with driving rain, below-freezing wind chill from near-gale-force winds, and even hail. The *Boston Globe* described it as "the worst weather ever at the Boston Marathon."

The Boston Marathon had always been held on a Monday, specifically Patriots' Day in the Commonwealth of Massachusetts. Back in Seattle at Brooks's headquarters, it was technically a workday, but most employees were focused on the iconic race unfolding in real time three thousand miles away. Many employees grabbed laptops and gathered in our Beastro common area for a Boston Marathon viewing party. Despite the enormity of this event, a monthly business review meeting had been ill-scheduled over top of the live race. Thirty or so of us sat in that

Brooks athlete Des Linden wins the 2018 Boston Marathon, becoming the first American woman to do so since 1985. She broke the tape more than 4 minutes ahead of the second-place finisher, on a race day that tested runners with driving rain, freezing temperatures, and near-gale-force winds. *Courtesy of Justin Britton*

meeting, distracted and a little anxious. Before long, it became clear most everyone's attention had switched from the presenter in the front of the room to their laptops and smartphones. Everyone was checking the live race results. When Des Linden took the lead with approximately four miles left, we knew the meeting was over. We finally asked the presenter to pause. We put the meeting agenda aside and asked a director who was sneaking peeks at the race to broadcast his laptop on the conference room's big screen. We were riveted. Des was wearing our Hyperion Elite shoes and our Canopy Jacket.

And she was running out front . . . alone.

Des broke the tape in 2:39:54, far from the course record and her own personal best, yet she finished more than four minutes ahead of the second-place finisher. It was a victory for Brooks and fans of distance running in the United States as Des became the first American woman to win since 1985. Keep showing up, indeed. Shadrack Biwott crossed the line in 2:18:35, coming in third place overall as the first male finisher for the United States.

→ Brooks Rises with Runners and Athletes of Different Abilities

In 2016, Chief of Staff Tamara Hills and I sat down in Brooks's Beastro common area with Beth Knox, a longtime friend and business partner who had led several large-scale community events with running races attached and Brooks often plugged in. Beth told us she'd taken a new position as the CEO of the Special Olympics USA Games to be held the summer of 2018 in Seattle primarily on the University of Washington campus, just two miles down the road from Brooks's headquarters. She understood our brand values and wanted Brooks to come aboard as a partner.

The games, which carried a rally cry to "Rise with Us," demonstrated the abilities of athletes with intellectual disabilities through world-class competition and promoted the ideals of inclusion through sport. It was an incredible opportunity for Brooks to demonstrate our values on all who run. We knew we had to be part of it.

Our partnership was multifaceted and leaned into our strengths around activating and connecting at events. Among other activities, our cross-departmental team designed a limited edition 2018 Special Olympics USA Games gear collection with a donation giveback component; brought Special Olympics athletes onto our Brooks Beasts competitive team; and created rich storytelling opportunities around athletes, gear, the broader Special Olympics community, and the power of sports to unite us all. In addition, more than three hundred Brooks employees volunteered at the games, bringing our energy and expressing our values human to human. It was an authentic partnership that resonated strongly with the running community and the four-thousand-plus athletes and coaches, hundred thousand on-site attendees, and half-million fans who watched live on ESPN and ABC over the six-day competition. It remains today one of the most poignant and proud moments for employees in expressing Brooks's commitment to support all who run.

→ 2019 Failure to Launch: Scaling a Business Is Not Linear

By year-end 2018, we had the wind at our back again. Our Brooks strategy was working and the momentum that began in July 2017 (two years after the entire category hit a wall) had accelerated. We pivoted to growth by adding new runners and posted record results with revenue of $644 million, up 26 percent, and new high-water marks for profits, return on capital, and market share, which now put Brooks at number two in the United States, with 12.7 percent share behind Nike.

Every year in March we put together a strategy offsite following the Pillsbury playbook with an agenda around future opportunities, trends, and developments to assess how to tune our Charting Brooks's Future plan. We would often engage our board of advisors on the strategy and would regularly invite a member to share his or her wisdom with us on relevant experiences. On our minds in 2019 was scaling for growth. I had learned that at seemingly every milestone in Brooks's growth, our systems, processes, and plans needed to be upgraded and retooled to execute at scale. This retooling included all of us as leaders. My job certainly had required me to change and grow as the company needed a CEO with completely different modes and skills at different stages. My role from $100 million to $300 million to $500 million had morphed dramatically based on what the company and the team needed. I was certain that successfully leading the team to scale would require me to evolve at $1 billion-plus.

So, in March 2019, I invited our new board member Darrell Cavens to speak to the senior leadership team on what scaling a business to $1 billion entailed. Darrell is a hall-of-fame-caliber entrepreneur who cofounded Zulily in Seattle and built the e-commerce company to $1 billion in sales in a little more than five years. Darrell was getting to know Brooks well and, like us, saw our opportunity. But he was curious if we knew what it would take to successfully scale for growth.

We sat around a large, rectangular meeting room table, welcoming the dinner dialogue after a full day of meetings. It was a lively evening with challenging discussions on our assumptions for building a strategy into plans that could deliver on our opportunity. Darrell was highly articulate on how things change as you grow. Complexity multiplies seemingly exponentially with success. It requires a step function in how you operate; a linear extrapolation of what you know and do today will not cut it. He couldn't get a bite of dinner as our leadership team grilled him with questions. He was challenging us to think more openly than we were about what it would take to execute well at scale. Little did we know our first lesson would begin in just six weeks.

In 2016 we launched a project to replace our Sumner, Washington, distribution center, which carried a lease set to expire in July 2019. From the beginning, this project focused on replicating and scaling Brooks's business model while driving down delivery times and costs. Key goals included a Midwest location to improve customer service levels, reduce freight and operational costs, and reduce our carbon footprint. A key success factor was to avoid any disruption whatsoever for customers. In a speech to the launch team in 2017, I explained that we were not to beta test new systems on our customers. We were all acutely aware of industry debacles that had occurred when competitors moved distribution centers, and we were determined Brooks would be an exception. It was clear that a troubled launch costs way more in customer and employee disruption than taking the time to get it right up front. For the project, the team selected strong, experienced partners to guide us on facilities development, warehouse management system design, and warehouse equipment and automation planning. We hired an expert consultant, JSC, to integrate it all.

We ultimately chose a location in Whitestown, Indiana, just outside Indianapolis. The supply chain optimization (SCO) project called for more than six months of testing to make certain the facility would be ready to operate without disruption. This seemed like overkill to me, but it was insurance against glitches that would affect customers at start-up.

Brooks's COO Holger Mueller architected the project but unfortunately was diagnosed with stage 4 prostate cancer in the summer of 2017. He was active early on, but as his treatment became more intense and his health deteriorated, the team began to pick up the slack. Sadly, he passed in December 2018. It was a huge loss for our team and devastating for his wife and three young boys. Holger had made incredible contributions to bring more focus and discipline to managing our business. His passing at such a young age was yet another reminder that life is short and you need to enjoy the journey along the way.

We were now five months out from our planned distribution center transition date. The SCO project's cross-functional team of some fifteen key leaders from all relevant departments stepped up to proceed against plan.

With more than two hundred tests completed and systems put under stress, all lights were green prior to changeover. Confidence was high. During this time, the project's steering committee briefly discussed operating two distribution centers simultaneously. The option was rejected due to the complexity of developing two inventories in the system and the potential customer disruption of receiving two separate shipments for the same order. This decision would prove to be a critical error.

Fortunately for Brooks, one of our longtime key leaders, Dan Sheridan, was promoted to COO to run our overall global business in early 2019. Dan joined Brooks in 1998 as a tech rep and had gone on to build our distribution strategy, develop our accounts, reimagine our grassroots tech rep program ("Brooks Gurus"), and architect our multichannel digital and e-commerce strategy. As COO, Dan was parachuting into his role just two months before the transition to our new DC. It would be a lesson in crisis management for all of us.

By the end of April 2019, we made the switch to our new facility in Indianapolis. By the end of the second week of May, we knew we had a monumental disaster on our hands. The automated systems were spec'd to ship forty-five thousand units per day with approximately seventy employees. Yet, we were shipping fewer than six thousand units per day. Our unfilled orders began to pile up. By July we had shipped about 50 percent of the orders we had for the second quarter. I began to refer to our new DC as Fort Knox. We had three million units in inventory in the racks and could not get them out. Each shoe box had figuratively two twenty-dollar bills in margin attached to them and our retailers were dumbfounded at our inability to just ship them out. It was gut wrenching to have the product to meet demand but not be able to ship it day after day.

This debacle was painful for a team that had always prided itself on hustling for our customers to consistently deliver on time and complete. Brooks had historically won nearly every service award from specialty and sporting goods retailers. We were proud of the trust we had created. This was a big black eye for us. It would be a six-month, all-hands-on-deck crisis to fix the problems and deliver the growth we had created in the market. How could we have allowed this to happen?

At the core, it was clear to me in the first month that this failure was a leadership error that started with me. We had built a new facility with new systems, automation, management, and employees, and we expected it to work. But it was destined to fail because the facility design had a critical flaw: it simply could not execute Brooks's unique business of large volume product launches to thousands of retailers in a two-week period coupled with thousands of daily small orders and e-commerce shipments that needed a one-day turnaround. Despite rigorous analysis and design promises from the "expert consultants," the design could do neither. We would have to unplug much of the system and manually work around the bottlenecks and flaws.

While these problems should have been foreseen, the real error was not running the two facilities simultaneously for at least six months. We took way too many risks that we did not properly assess. In the early weeks as we struggled, people began to point fingers at each other, trying to find what or whom to blame. Knowing that would be wasted energy, I publicly took responsibility for the debacle with our employees, our customers, and our owner. It was painful but truthful and necessary.

When we closed the books on 2019, we actually posted 3.5 percent growth with revenue, hitting $667 million. Profits were basically flat compared to the previous year, but we left some $70 million in orders unfulfilled. By year-end, we had more than three hundred people working in three shifts in a facility that was intended to require only seventy people on one shift to deliver our demand. It was a humbling and hard lesson. Scaling our business would not be linear and would indeed require a step function in capability. Darrell Cavens's instincts just nine months earlier had been prescient.

→ 2020: No Playbook for a Global Pandemic

We entered 2020 with an aggressive plan and strong momentum as our fourth quarter 2019 results were back to double-digit, profitable growth, and we were largely delivering demand and catching up on meeting our service promises. We had a plan to hit nearly $770 million in revenue and were confident in our products, brand positioning, marketing engine, and team. But we would need to execute well. The Indianapolis distribution center debacle had us hyper focused on execution across the team. That January, I had a call with IDEO's Clark Scheffy, who was canvassing CEOs on their outlook for the new decade. I shared with him that the global economy was strong and with the tax cuts of 2018, the US economy went from solid growth to turbocharged. But it felt somewhat like 2008—things were spinning so fast, it seemed unsustainable. I was concerned there would be a black swan–level event as characterized today by many in business as a rare, unpredictable, and catastrophic occurrence with global consequences. There was plenty to be concerned about including global trade tensions, currency stability, high debt levels, political instability, income inequality, climate change, racism, increasing violence, and weakening institutions.

But a global pandemic was not on my mind.

2020 was to be an Olympic year with the marathon trials happening in late February in Atlanta and the track and field trials
scheduled for June in Eugene, Oregon. For the marathon trials,
we hosted our athletes, coaches, influencers, retailers, and media partners for several days of panels and discussions on all
things running and Brooks including: "What Des Wore" at Boston, highlighting our Canopy Jacket; the early version of our
Hyperion Racing shoe; "20 Years of Hansons ODP" with Keith
and Kevin Hanson; and an outlook for the sport and the industry with Brooks staff and key retailers from across the United
States. We took over a downtown Atlanta venue we dubbed "Hyperion House" that was blocks from the start and finish line of
the Saturday morning race. The top three male and female winners would represent the United States in Tokyo.

Brooks athletes did not place in the top three. Des Linden
just missed, coming in fourth with a time of 2:29:03. It nonetheless was her fourteenth sub-2:30 marathon, an American record. Clayton "CJ" Albertson was the first Brooks male athlete
to finish, coming in seventh with a time of 2:11:49. Brooks
showed well overall with more than 10 percent of athletes on
course wearing the new Hyperion 2 shoe with a carbon spring
and a nitrogen-infused midsole.

The Atlanta trials were an incredible and exciting start of the
year for the sport, the industry, and for Brooks. A few days later,
as everyone in the world knows, COVID-19 stopped us all in our
tracks. Every person, family, and business would have to navigate
the rapidly spreading virus that was clearly lethal to some people
and made many others very sick. Because the virus was novel, all
of us were learning in real time. In late February, Seattle would
record the first confirmed COVID-19 death in the United States.
Fear began to spread. How was it transmitted? How lethal was
it? How do we protect ourselves from transmission?

The COVID-19 pandemic created rolling health and economic dual crises globally. With Brooks's global supply chain

and distribution footprint, we watched this virus move through China, Europe, and then North America and observed its impact on people and business. With stores closed and demand depressed, the entire cash cycle froze, with e-commerce sales the exception. When stores closed in Europe in mid-March, Brooks EMEA (Europe, Middle East, and Africa) Managing Director Matt Dodge created a working plan to navigate through the crisis. He labeled it "Recover to Run." We adopted it globally with the first step to understand COVID-19's impact on running participation and demand.

Brooks's leadership team stepped up to bring our employees along in support of our Recover to Run plan. Despite a remote working mode that—little did we know—would still be in place one year later, our teams and processes have remained focused and functioning through the disruption and have been key to our ability to execute. In April, when the outcome for people and businesses was murky and uncertain, we were cutting production schedules to stop the huge fire hose of inventory.

Berkshire Hathaway ownership was a strong advantage for Brooks in navigating these uncertain times. The cash-flow crisis was real and the expectation was made clear that we should live off of our own balance sheet. Berkshire was there if we ran out of cash, but we would manage the business as if we owned it. Vice Chairman Greg Abel was managing all of the noninsurance businesses for Warren. I created an update for Greg on our Recover to Run plan and all the decisions we were trying to assess to survive phase 1 of the pandemic economic shock and get to the other side when we knew runners would be running and retail would recover in some form. Greg shared what other Berkshire businesses were seeing and what they were doing to survive, including dramatic cost cutting and downsizing to get costs in line with the new reality. His advice to me was to "follow your customer." This was key guidance as it gave me the confidence and courage to be patient with layoffs and cutbacks until we could see how the pandemic would impact our sport and the fitness regimen that running provides. So many CEOs in our industry, my peer network, and the media were seeing the pandemic as an opportunity to "cut out the deadwood" with the assumption that every organization has people or initiatives that ought to be terminated, but in normal times complacency or laziness prevented organizations from taking action.

This was not the case at Brooks. We spent years building our teams, recruiting key talent across our organization from the crazy competitive market in Seattle and our running industry. Meanwhile, we had worked hard to develop our people and align all employees around our strategy, plans, and values. While layoffs are never pleasant for anyone, I wanted to protect our years of investment in our team. Everything good for our customers and our business comes from the daily efforts, creativity, passion, and dedication of a thousand employees. Each and every one was rowing an oar. It was a nail biter to think about going backward several years on the team-building progress we had made.

→ Customer Obsession Requires Courage with Conviction

We believed there was a good chance people would keep running through the pandemic. We had seen this happen when the Great Recession hit and running became part of coping with tough times. Health and wellness were front of mind; running, walking, and hiking outdoors were all social distance and fresh-air-friendly activities. Might participation actually increase?

With retailers, the sport, and road races all closed, we were not getting the demand signals we were used to. Our team sprang into action to create a runner participation and product demand model from all new signals. Our Run Sights Lab created focus groups seeking a read on changes in current runners' habits and people who had just started since the shutdowns. As well, our team compiled all of the activity data we could find from industry sources and companies including Strava. Our in-market Brooks Gurus set up in high traffic parks at the same time every day and counted the number of runners. We analyzed weekly sales data in the United States on 80 percent of our distribution and tracked digital sales versus in-store sales.

Our operations team took all of these new signals and built a demand plan that gave us the confidence to reignite production and build inventory for year-over-year growth. By mid-May, we were confident we were seeing growth again. We were diligently creating more precision in our runner signal modeling. It was a critical advantage for us that spoke to our laser focus on the runner. It would have been much harder to forecast causal, fashion, or lifestyle product, but in running, activity drives purchase and our obsession gave us an advantage in moving quickly.

We would make other key decisions that proved to be important not only for surviving the early shock of the stay-at-home orders, but also for remaining agile and assessing demand to recover quickly. While all of our grassroots, event-sports marketing, and retail marketing were paused, we decided to increase our investments in digital demand creation with runners, driving engagement online when they were ready to shop. Our product teams continued to drive development calendars while merchandising trimmed the line to core styles and colors. Sales and operations planning teams stepped up to lead an integrated, enterprise-level focus driven by runner signals. The result was aggressive moves to manage production to demand and secure capacity for 2021 growth. We executed weekly town halls through the early summer to engage employees, partners, and sales teams on our opportunities, realities, actions, and beliefs as we moved through the Recover to Run plan. Navigating the uncertain early days of the pandemic well was an outcome of Greg Abel's edict to follow our customer. Once we saw the demand, we were able to move boldly.

→ Systemic Racism Laid Bare

On top of the health and economic challenges, a third crisis arose in the second quarter with the senseless deaths of Ahmaud Arbery, George Floyd, Breonna Taylor, and more, creating protests and discussions on equal justice and the reality of structural, systemic racism in America. Many employees and others in the running community demanded points of view from Brooks as a purpose-driven brand and as a company that champions the run as the world's most inclusive sport. We stepped up to communicate our values and actions internally and on social media channels. We were committed to be a bold advocate for inclusion for all in running. It was not only the right thing to do but a way to grow our sport.

Due to our intense focus on runners, Brooks successfully navigated the global pandemic and related economic contraction in 2020—a year that will forever be etched in our memories given its unexpected challenges—posting nearly $850 million in revenue, up 27 percent despite a global pandemic. That was an all-time record. Better yet, we came out well positioned to address the growth in running and gain market share.

Our 2020 success is best viewed in context of the last several years from our Performance Is Timeless declaration in 2016. This pivot set Brooks on a path to win with runners (see figure 15).

As we entered 2021, we had more optimism than ever on the power of the run to make a person's day better. The pandemic had brought increased attention on personal health and exercise. Running was ready to play its central role. Brooks was built for the energy you feel in the aftermath of a good run. Because we followed our customer and did not lay off people, cut

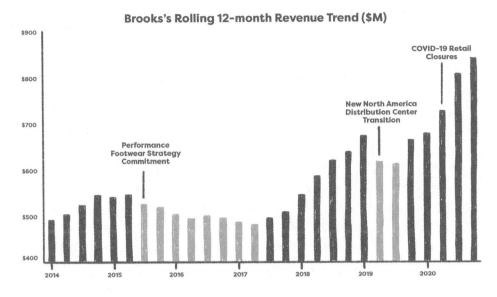

Figure 15

marketing, or unravel our supply chain partnerships, we carried industry-leading momentum into this new decade.

At our annual all-employee virtual meeting in February, we relived the roller-coaster year and celebrated the successes we had created. Then we presented our 2021 plans for Brooks, forecasting $1 billion in global revenue. In the coming year, we would fulfill our crazy ambition for the brand articulated a decade earlier.

CHAPTER 9

Hitting a Wall: Fighting Cancer

O**N NOVEMBER 6, 2017, I WAS ONSTAGE** giving the opening keynote to several hundred people at our global sales meeting in Seattle. Brooks had turned the corner and was set to have a record year in 2018. The brand was getting hot and the company was firing on all cylinders. I had the honor of inviting Gabe Grunewald up to the stage to interview her on her epic journey as a professional runner while fighting a rare cancer for the previous eight years. Brooks signed Gabe as one of the most vibrant young talents on the track from the University of Minnesota. She went on to compete at the highest levels around the world, winning a US title and crushing 1500-meter and 3000-meter races. All the while, Gabe lived two public lives: one as a runner and another as a cancer fighter and activist. She was first diagnosed with adenoid cystic carcinoma as a student athlete at the University of Minnesota in 2009. At times she was so sick she couldn't run a step. But Gabe remained a tenacious competitor and an inspiration with her grit and positive spirit until her passing in 2019.

Little did I know that just thirty-one days after that keynote, I would officially join Gabe in the cancer club.

For several months I had not been feeling well. I had heartburn that would not go away. I was borderline sick with fatigue and weakness that never left. I'd signed up that fall for the University of Washington Dawg Dash 10K, an annual Brooks-sponsored fun run on campus. I had always scored my races by how I felt at the end, and this one by any measure was my worst ever. I had to walk the hills and just couldn't muster the energy to finish strong. Something was wrong. It was time to see the doctor.

After several weeks of tests to eliminate likely possibilities from stomach ailments, acid reflux, and ulcers, I was finally scheduled for an endoscopy to take a closer look. It's an inpatient procedure under anesthetic. My wife, MaryEllen, and I went to Overlake Hospital on Thursday, December 7. Mine was the last procedure of the day. Soon I was waking up in a recovery chair. From my space, I could see the doctor on the phone, chatting with patients who were in before me and communicating the results of their tests. I caught his eyes across the nurse's station, and he quickly looked down and continued his rounds. I had a sense that he looked more serious in that instant than I might expect. As he approached us at about 4:45 that afternoon with my test images in his hand, his face was expressionless as he delivered the message directly.

"I have bad news for you," he said. "You have an approximately 2-inch tumor at the junction of your esophagus and your stomach. I am 99 percent sure it's cancer, more specifically esophageal cancer, and you are going to need a surgeon." The gravity of those words hit hard. My brother had died of brain cancer. But before I went there, I looked at my wife. I could see MaryEllen's face drop, suddenly stricken with sadness and fear. The doctor had already been on the phone with surgeons at the University of Washington, and he would be referring us to one of them. I would find out that UW was a national center in treatment for this cancer and, in fact, had pioneered many of the procedures in the past thirty years. Not only did they have a team approach with chemotherapy and radiation oncologists, but their association with the Seattle Cancer Care Alliance (SCCA) benefited from a relationship with the world-renowned Fred Hutchinson Cancer Research Center, also in Seattle. Each year, surgeons at UW performed more than seventy of the complex esophagectomy procedures that I would need.

→ Joining the Cancer Club

When I got home, I did what I always do when a family member or a friend comes to me with the news that they were diagnosed with cancer. I jumped on the internet to research esophageal cancer and related treatments including the esophagectomy surgical procedure. As is often the case, the five-year survival rate was low. I now had a 20 percent probability of being here in five years, as only one in five people on average make it that far. Equally daunting, an esophagectomy is an incredibly complex surgical procedure and often makes the top ten list of those to avoid. I had an appointment with the care team at UW for the following week, so we had the weekend for all of this to sink in. On doctor's orders, I was now on a liquid diet, as the tumor was creating blockage risk. We stopped by the grocery store and bought a weekend's supply of Ensure.

I had joined a club no one wants to join, but a club that is comfortingly and reassuringly supportive of its members. Once your diagnosis is known, its subcategory membership comes out of the woodwork to share stories and offer help. When I would stop by the Brooks Beastro, once employees knew my news, colleagues would come up to tell me about their own stories or that of their husband, wife, or friend who beat the odds. A club, yes, and it is also a brother- and sisterhood.

A longtime Brooks athlete and employee, Silvia Ruegger, was diagnosed with the same cancer I had around the same time. A Canadian, she held her nation's marathon record for twenty-eight years. She won the Houston and Pittsburgh Marathons and competed for Canada in the 1984 Olympics. I had been incredibly inspired by her over the years. She was on a mission to support girls' and women's running, helping Brooks create our Moving Comfort sports bras. Sadly, she lost her battle with cancer in 2019.

MaryEllen called our three boys and let them in on the news. It was a major shock to process in the moment, but that is what we all now had to do. As I would begin to personally absorb the news, at one level I was at peace. I have been so fortunate in my life to have a job at Brooks that fulfilled all of my career hopes and goals. In being part of a team and building a brand, I felt I had my dream job. I've had great mentors and made many wonderful friendships along the way. Moreover, I had been married to MaryEllen for thirty-five years, and in fact we had been best friends for nearly forty years. I was immensely proud of our boys and the lives they were building for themselves. Best of all, my eldest son, Michael, and his wife, Kacey, had two children, Teagan and Declan; my middle son, Joel, and his wife, Marisa, gave us a third grandchild, Lennon; and my youngest son, Reid, was on a good track in life. I was so grateful for the life that I had and was concluding I had no regrets.

As mentioned before, when times get tough, people's true values are often revealed. I was forced to stress test this theory in earnest. As I processed my situation, I knew I did not want to live in fear, even for one day. The journey ahead was full of unknowns, but I believed to my core that life is about the journey, and I wanted to get the most out of every day, no matter how many days were left. What do I mean by life is a journey? For me, it's not about the finish line. It's about the satisfaction that comes from all that it took to reach the finish line. I have found that once you get a win, the satisfaction of it, in and of itself, is fleeting. I love to win, but I know that a truly happy and meaningful life comes from the relationships with people you engage with along the way.

One of the most influential books I've ever read is *Man's Search for Meaning* by Viktor Frankl, who chronicled his life in Nazi concentration camps during World War II. The way a prisoner imagines his future affects his ability to survive. Frankl observes that life is not just about happiness but also about meaning and impact. Do you live in fear for what you might lose or do you fight for what could be? I've always chosen not to live in fear but to look forward because I want to be there tomorrow—for my boys, for my grandkids, for my wife, and for the people with whom I work.

On reflection, I quickly concluded that I was doing exactly what I wanted to be doing at this point in my life. I had no interest in shrinking my world or retiring to travel or play golf or whatever. I wanted to keep living all the facets of my life for as long as I could.

I also knew that I did not want to be defined by cancer; I did not want it to dominate my life. I wanted to be me—the CEO, teammate, husband, Dad, Papa, runner, lapsed hockey player, board member, friend. I did not want to carry daily fear of my cancer or of what I had to lose. The truth is I had a lot to lose, but getting fixated on that had zero value as I saw it. It would take me into sadness and bitterness. It would sap energy and time that I could be putting into the things I enjoyed in life.

While I was coming to terms with my situation, I quickly saw that it was actually a bigger emotional blow to my wife and our boys. It was one thing for me to accept my cancer at a rational level, but the idea that they—and our grandkids—might have to go on without me was where the fear of loss was anchored, and it was impossible to ignore. I decided right then and there to fight with all I had for as many years as possible. I needed to beat this cancer and be part of the 20 percent who survive it beyond five years.

I needed a plan.

Once I got through the shock and the fear, I quickly started framing out a plan. Over the years, whenever I was in a tough spot without a clear path, I was often anxious to the point of not being able to sleep. Whether it was in business or in life, once a problem presented itself, urgency kicked in and my brain went to work on solving for a plan. It was clear that treatment would need to become my first priority. I believed what I preached: Everything good in life comes from being healthy. I needed to focus on getting this cancer out of my body.

Just two days after the diagnosis, my anxious thoughts turned to Brooks. How was I going to handle this with my team? I've always been all-in at work, so any change in my schedule or health would be impossible to hide. I would be going to treatments every day and knew well the effects of chemo and radiation would likely include extreme fatigue, nausea, and losing my hair. I had already begun to lose weight, and getting enough calories in during chemo would be an additional challenge.

Worse yet, what if I was unable to work at all for some or all of this treatment plan? What if I had to take a medical leave of several months? Would I still have a job? Would the company have to move on for its own benefit and that of the team? That would be a horrible outcome for me. I could beat the cancer after a tough fight and be on the other side at age fifty-eight with no job, sitting at home. The prospect of being off the team was a scary one for me.

The first call I made to help think through how to communicate and navigate my health issue at Brooks was to Charlotte Guyman, who was both on Brooks's board of advisors and on Berkshire Hathaway's board. She had also previously chaired the UW Medical Center board and helped confirm I was in the right place with the right team for my cancer care. Charlotte was empathic and supportive. She was certain Warren Buffett would be, too.

On Sunday morning, day three, I called Warren to discuss my predicament and my likely treatment plan, and to get his advice on how to manage Brooks during treatment. I also wanted to share my fear that I would recover only to have lost the job that I loved. He had a lot to share on being transparent with everyone on my cancer—there was no value in hiding it. He had just worked through treatment for prostate cancer the year before and so had experience with the fatigue that comes with radiation and chemo treatments. Warren recommended I look at how Jamie Dimon, CEO at JPMorgan Chase, had handled the communication after he was diagnosed with throat cancer. In the end, Warren suggested I make getting well the priority, communicate openly with the Brooks team that I would be in treatment, and not to worry: My job would be waiting for me when I was healthy on the other side.

With the support from Warren and Charlotte, I penned the Brooks senior leadership team an email that Sunday afternoon:

December 10, 2017

Hello all,

I am sorry to interrupt your Sunday, but I want you to know some personal news that could not wait. Last Thursday I had a procedure that discovered a significant tumor in my esophagus/ stomach that we are 99 percent certain to be cancer. I have more tests coming up this week and am meeting with doctors on Thursday to begin a plan for treatment. It will certainly include surgery and likely chemotherapy and radiation. This was of course a shock to me and my family. Since October 1st I have been not quite right. But then again, running more slowly has been a trend for a long time! I never considered it could be more than a seasonal ailment, but life is a journey so here I go.

If I could choose, I would keep this to myself, hunker down and beat this. My hockey player instincts lead me to a mode of dogged determination, focus, persistence and a never quit attitude. But . . . I am part of a team and treatment is going to take time from my daily schedule to deal with. Until I get to this coming Friday, I am not sure what that will look like for the next 60 to 90 days. My desire would be to stay in my role and manage my treatment as necessary. Less travel, more empowerment and delegation as I will be missing meetings. Exactly what my mode will be is too early to say.

I have discussed my situation with Warren and Charlotte and both are supportive. I am proud to be part of the Brooks team and I love this Company. I ask for your support during this next chapter of my life. I am inspired by Gabe Grunewald and hope that I can be nearly as brave as she.

My tests and doctor visits this week will have me out Tuesday 7–10AM, Thursday 12:45–5PM and Friday 7–11AM. Until I know more Friday, I would ask that you keep this to just our senior team. I know that once I start treatment it is not realistic to hide it so I will cross that bridge next week and communicate more broadly with the team.

Thanks in advance for your understanding.

Jim

On Thursday of that week, I met with the team of doctors who would lead me through my upcoming battle. The plan would include a seven-week regimen of chemotherapy infusions starting in January, coupled with twenty-seven daily proton radiation therapy treatments, all designed to attack the cancer cells and in particular those that may have spread to my system.

Next, I would rest for eight weeks so that my body could recover and regain strength. In early April, I would have the six-hour surgery to remove the tumor along with most of my esophagus and replumb my digestive system. I would be in the hospital for eight days and then recover at home for four to six weeks. As with any aggressive treatment strategy and complex surgery, there were risks and uncertainties around all of this, but it felt good to have a plan and be guided by a team that does this every day and were among the best in the world.

By the end of the first week, I had a clear treatment plan from my doctors, complete support from my boss, and confidence that my team would not only have my back but would keep Brooks on track with the hard-earned momentum we had created. Next, I had my best friend and life partner, MaryEllen, at my side for what would be a daily team effort for the next five months. And finally, I had the love and emotional support of my boys, my family, and my friends. I felt so fortunate to have so much support as I prepared to start treatment in the new year.

We hit the ground running with my first chemo infusion on January 4 at 8:30 in the morning. In a routine that would become familiar, I would do a weekly blood draw and then be in a room for approximately four hours for an infusion of two chemotherapy drugs. Every weekday evening, I would travel to a proton radiation therapy session at about 8:00. They put tattoo markers in the center of my chest and then hit me with a targeted radiation beam aimed at the tumor. It was a dance shuffle—one step chemo, four steps radiation every week for seven straight weeks.

I was able to continue working all the way through this treatment on a limited schedule. I had secured the last radiation appointments of the day so that I could work about five hours each day, get some sleep afterward and then head to the hospital for treatment. Severe fatigue began to set in from the chemo and radiation (it was never clear which was more responsible). I came to refer to my condition as a "chemo-coma." Its mission was to kill cancer cells, but it was also making me pretty sick overall. I would lose fifteen pounds, but not my hair.

By mid-February I had completed the radiation and chemo treatments and would rest up for surgery scheduled for the first week of April. I worked through this rest period and even managed to include a long, fantastic weekend in Carmel, California, with our kids and grandkids. The support of my family was a true gift. All three boys came into town for my surgery, and we had a great dinner the night before I entered the hospital. I refer to this as my "last supper" with a cancerous digestive system, because just twenty-four hours later it would be gone and I would have a new one. Fasting lay ahead for surgery, but that night I was grateful to have my wife and three boys around the table enjoying great conversation and a locally sourced steak.

The six-hour surgery was deemed a success, and MaryEllen and the boys went out for dinner and drinks to toast my recovery. I spent eight days on my first-ever visit as a patient to a hospital. The team approach to care was impressive, but the trauma from surgery was intense. I had seven tubes in me, and the goal by week's end was to be rid of them and have all of my systems back functioning independently. The doctors and nurses posted a daily schedule on a white board that included walking laps around the floor. It wasn't a track but it'd have to do. I would take my "tree" of tubes and drugs and push it with my walker, often with MaryEllen's arm.

I entered the hospital with the goal of not being that patient from hell. My dad had passed a few years earlier, and my brothers and sisters had relayed how he had an angry rant with his young cardiologist who dared to suggest that he quit his daily intake of alcohol to help recover from bypass surgery. I was determined not to be that angry, bitter, selfish patient that nurses and staff would try to avoid. The care at UW was outstanding and on sleepless evenings the nurses would compliment my Gregory Alan Isakov music mixes to which my son Reid had introduced me.

A pleasant surprise on day three of post-op was a gift from Warren Buffett, a five-pound box of See's Candies. My first reaction was, really? I was on a feeding tube—it would be weeks before I could eat any solid food. What was he thinking? But on opening the card, the move was a Warren classic: "Jim—I am sure you are getting great care at UW Hospital so put these out on the nurse's station as a thank you and let them know if your great care continues, there is more where this came from!" Needless to say, Warren's sentiment gained me points with the staff.

Among all the family and friends, cards and well wishes, my team at Brooks sent along something I still have today. It was a hockey stick signed by dozens of my fellow teammates at Brooks with words of encouragement. It motivated me to get through the week in the hospital and yearn to be back in the game once I recovered.

The highlight of the week was an active X-ray scan to check my new digestive system. I was on a platform that would shift me from prone to upright while I drank a contrast solution, and they could watch it transfer into my stomach. The doctor came out and proclaimed, "Great news, no leaks!" I was headed home to recover. I would be on a feeding tube for a few weeks or as long as it took until my new system was able to handle enough calories eating solids. The cancer was out of my body, and my thoughts shifted to getting stronger and healthy.

→ Back to Work

Meanwhile the world continued to surge ahead. Along with my new feeding tube, I flew to the Berkshire Hathaway annual meeting in Nebraska, and then a few days later gave the keynote at the Brooks sales meeting at a hotel not far from my home. It was early May and our North American sales team had not seen me since my surgery, radiation, and chemo. I was still regaining strength and probably looked like a shadow of my former self. Six months earlier, at the previous sales meeting in November, I had interviewed Gabe Grunewald onstage about her cancer, not realizing at the time that I too had cancer in my body. There were hundreds of people in the hotel ballroom when Dan Sheridan kicked off the meeting that May morning.

I would later learn that Dan was nervous because he wanted to acknowledge the elephant in the room, but also didn't want to overdo it. He simply said, "I'd like to introduce the toughest person I know." I was startled by the response as the room erupted and just continued to get louder. I so appreciated their welcoming me back, but as the ovation went on I was a bit uncomfortable being the center of attention. I saw a few tears, a lot of positive energy, and for some time, I couldn't even get a word out. I was really moved and when it died down, I simply jumped into the keynote I had prepared. The theme for the meeting was "Accelerate," and that was exactly what I intended to do, and exactly what I needed our team to do. I love to bring energy to these talks, and I did, but I also felt the lingering effects of fighting cancer for the past five months. I easily grew tired and would need rest at various points during the day. Not only did the team reenergize me, but we also flew Des Linden in for the meeting after her historic win in the Boston Marathon. What a great time it was to be at Brooks.

→ Running My Way to Recovery

I had always loved playing hockey, a tough gym workout, or a good six-mile run. Even though it was often physically taxing, somehow my body knew the soreness and fatigue was good for me and I felt healthy and alive afterward. I knew what endorphins were and I wanted them back after being sick for nine months. Inspired by Gabe Grunewald to be brave, I intended to use running to get healthy, keep the cancer away, and get fit.

I needed to rebuild my core after the trauma of the surgery and for the first time in my life I had no fitness base. I had to start from scratch. I needed a holistic plan given the work I had in front of me.

Enter Brooks team member Hannah Schultz in the summer of 2018. Hannah was a manager on our footwear team and like so many people at Brooks was a runner and athlete. Back in the day, she had competed as a 400-meter sprinter and had recently competed regionally in the American Ninja Warrior program. Prior to Brooks, she had earned a degree in exercise science and had extensive coaching experience. We started in the gym and added the dirt track at Green Lake for morning workouts. Surgery trauma was a new factor I had never dealt with. It was incredibly hard and painful. By August I was adding in one-mile intervals at a ten-minute pace.

But the truth was, my body was not happy. It almost seemed like the more effort I put in, the more my body resisted it. The nausea following any significant exertion was new for me. It is part of competitive running after a grueling 800-meter race, but I had never experienced that. In August my doctors suggested I take a break from running, so we focused on the gym. In January 2019, I had a CT scan and had good news: no sign of cancer. Unfortunately, my doctor found a new problem that for me would be more devastating than the initial cancer diagnosis.

→ Beating Cancer but Losing More

The CT scan showed clearly that in the nine months since surgery, my left lung had elevated nearly eight inches and moved up into my chest cavity. My left diaphragm was paralyzed from damage to my phrenic nerve during the esophagectomy. This was one of the many remote risks of my surgery. I had been unlucky. This powerful muscle that had been cycling for fifty-eight years with every breath now had no nerve to fire it.

Since the day of my surgery the muscle had stopped working. Over the coming months, it would atrophy, thin out, be pushed north by my other organs, and compress my left lung. Tests confirmed that my lung capacity was 56 percent of average for my age. Essentially I had one lung, and my recent struggles running now made sense. Every month that went by, my aerobic capacity was shrinking.

After waiting a year to see if there was any regeneration of the nerve, I opted for another major surgery to tighten my left diaphragm, reinflate the lung, and hope for more aerobic capacity. With fitness being my true lifelong hobby, I wanted to have as much giddyup in my system as possible for my remaining years on this earth. The surgery was way more painful and as disruptive as the first. They removed a rib and made multiple folds in the diaphragm, then sutured it as tightly as possible before reinflating the lung. In my three-day hospital stay this go-around, my pain level was, for the first time in my life, ten on a scale of ten. The recovery was also lengthy as my core again had to be rebuilt, and I had more nerve damage in my rib cage that took six months to subside.

It is hard for me to describe what I have lost from this experience, but it is significant. When I see a friend, I am often asked, "How are you doing?" The answer is complicated, given my journey.

First, I am still challenged every day with my Frankenstein digestive system. Post-surgery, eating is always an adventure as my capacity is less, so smaller meals are key. I have tested many foods through trial and elimination plus had the help of an expert nutritionist. Nonetheless, I often still end up sick after eating, and it seems to be a physical systems issue. I feel best when I don't eat. My digestive system needs gravity; I have to sleep on a 30-degree pillow wedge so I don't wake up choking. My brain says I am hungry but my system has such limited capacity and gets easily upset so I pay for it if I listen to my hunger. I have not felt un-sick for more than a few days since my cancer symptoms presented in September 2017.

Next, the surgery trauma has left chronic discomfort in my ribs and abdomen. When I push myself running or in a workout, my body still registers as injured so I have yet to experience anything approaching endorphins. I am conflicted: Should I listen to my body and ease off or ignore the pain and try to re-wire my brain to power through it? This has been hard to discern as I used to know that pushing my body was a sure path to feeling strong, fit, and fast (relatively speaking, of course!). Yet the pain has me curtailing the intensity or missing days because of my digestive issues.

Finally, my aerobic capacity was never great, but it has been decimated by my cancer journey. I am now back in the gym and grateful that I am able to walk, hike, skate, ski, cycle, and run a bit. My running regimen includes one-minute intervals on the treadmill and walk/hike/runs with intervals until I am out of breath. At the same time, all athletes can track their current performance against their past. It is super humbling for me to think about that as I can't sustain a running heart rate without getting winded. While I hope to, I am not sure that I will "run" a full 5K again. It is hard for me not to think about the things I dearly miss, like a six-mile rave run on a sunny day in a beautiful place listening to my Bob Dylan Zen run mix.

→ The Gift of Playing Another Day

I remind myself that the most important result is that cancer is out of my body. I was fortunate on several fronts, not the least of which was the support of my family and my friends. The good news began with the fact that my cancer was operable. I also lived in a community that built and supported the University of Washington Medical Center, where Carlos A. Pellegrini, M.D., pioneered the initial techniques for the minimally invasive treatment of esophageal motility disorders, which helped me enormously.

Nearly four years out from my diagnosis, I believe the cancer is gone. I wake up every day with no thought or fear of it. I assume it was all removed, and I will beat the 20 percent odds as I approach year five. I am so grateful for the technology, doctors, and staff at UW and SCCA I had access to. It does not escape me that only sixty years ago, this esophageal cancer was not operable, and I would not have survived. I will have CT scans annually checking for the cancer's return but thus far each one has led to a high-five with my doctor. Cancer free!

I am also grateful because I have a lot and I can look ahead. I am here enjoying my family, my work, my friends, and the pure joy of (now four!) grandchildren. I know every day I have is a gift and my task is to soak in the moments each day presents. Joy, happiness, and meaning are not waiting at the finish line of life but come from the journey you are on with your family, teammates, friends, and people you meet along the way. Even if I can only run short sprints or intervals, I want to make them Run Happy moments.

Two weeks after my second surgery, I turned sixty years old. At a party with family and friends, I stood to share a few thoughts on life and the things I know to be true:

> We all need to enjoy the journey. Happiness in life does not really come from outcomes. I focused on them as much as anyone but came to know that life is about soaking in the journey every day with the people around you. Purpose and joy come in working with people and being present for them—day in, day out.
>
> Finally, be active every day—it delivers positive energy that makes everything else better. Have Cheetos at least once a month . . . and find time to laugh and have fun.
>
> Life is good . . .

CHAPTER 10

Filling the "White Space" with Trust

I **N STRATEGY DEVELOPMENT, WE TAKE A BLANK** sheet of paper or stand at a whiteboard and sketch out where a company might have room to maneuver in competing for customers on a crowded field. That "white space" on the page or board is an opportunity, a gap, an unmet or even unexpressed customer need. It is how we at Brooks developed our strategies to win in run, from product to distribution to brand. More broadly across society today, I believe *trust* is a white-space opportunity for every leader and business to fill.

It should come as no surprise that the average twenty-five-year-old does not trust leaders or the system; according to the Pew Research Center, nearly half of people ages 18 to 29 reported low trust overall. There is white-space opportunity for trust everywhere. My generation grew up with lapses in the truth that had great consequences. From the misinformation on the Vietnam War and Nixon's Watergate cover-up to false claims on weapons of mass destruction in Iraq, unprincipled self-interest is all around us. We've made progress in places, but under my Baby Boom generation's watch, we have gone sideways in so many others and have lost sight of our purpose, values, and promises.

We see cheating in business: the Wells Fargo sales culture, which offered incentives to systemically enroll unsuspecting customers in unwanted financial services. Volkswagen's secret use of diesel emissions "defeat devices" while claiming to be efficient and green. Facebook's complicity in selling personal information to Cambridge Analytica for use in targeting political ads. Corner-cutting on safety at Boeing with its 737 Max. Theranos and Elizabeth Holmes selling total fiction to at-risk patients.

We also see cheating in sports: the Houston Astros stealing pitch signs via video on their way to a World Series victory. The New England Patriots deflating balls and filming the other teams' practices. Lance Armstrong winning seven Tour de France championships while cheating with a systemic doping system. Track and Field has a sordid history of doping scandals, including the 100-meter Olympic event. And in running, it matters because cheating can work. Multiple studies point to a 4 percent to 10 percent improvement from testosterone and other performance-enhancing drugs. For example, Regina Jacobs won the 2003 World Indoor Championships 1500-meter in a time of 4:01.67. A 4 percent difference equates to 9.3 seconds, which if added to this finish time would have placed her eighth (second to last). Six months after this world championship victory, Jacobs tested positive for BALCO's designer steroid THG and was banned from competition for four years.

We see cheating across society: wealthy parents bribing university officials for a "side door" to higher education enrollment for their children. Cover-ups in the Catholic Church of priests' immoral and illegal behavior at the expense of children's safety and long-term psychological well-being. The quest to hold power at the expense of good governance, democratic principles, and citizens' interests culminating in events like the January 6, 2021, insurrection at the US Capitol, and Michigan state officials' dismantling Flint's water system, poisoning its residents.

The degradation of trust over time has been well covered and documented by many including by Edelman in their annual Edelman Trust Barometer. The cumulative effect of the disturbing events we've witnessed in recent decades has chipped away at trust in institutions, organizations, and leaders. In each case, there were clear choices for people to do the right thing. It might be a tough decision to make the right call in the moment, but too many did not. To be a trustable person, teammate, and leader, we need to think carefully about what is right. Discuss it, weigh it, and then do it. In my view, there is ample opportunity to lead and play the game within the lines, without an illegal or unethical advantage. Our civilized society is full of rules and laws for sports, justice, human rights, and economic activity plus ethical and moral norms for interacting with people. Playing by the rules and being accountable is essential to earn trust.

→ Filling the "White Space" for Trust as a Business

It is not lost on me that the weakness in our institutions of government and religion are a principal reason that businesses are being asked to step into the vacuum where they never have before. This is difficult in concept as businesses are essentially legally required and incentivized by the profit mandate to address all relevant customers without regard to politics, religion, gender, national origin, or race. Businesses are structured to be "for" things in the affirmative. When a business chooses to take a position "against" an issue in society, a major challenge becomes how to follow through with actions over time to support its statements and words.

In our connected world of over 7.5 billion people, the number of issues and problems demanding attention is overwhelming for any one person or business. Most if not all of us have personal passion about issues in the world, but I believe that businesses will make more impact when they focus on where their voice and resources have standing with their core stakeholders. From the start of my tenure as CEO, Brooks has committed to a purpose, values, and initiatives to welcome and include everyone into the sport of running and be responsible for our impact on the planet. Our employees and partners expect to know where our brand and business stand. Runners deserve to understand the foundation of the brand they buy and wear. Our purpose and values are meaningless, however, if they are not stated clearly, lived fully, tested, and reinforced. That is how trust is built and strengthened over time.

At Brooks, I know I must maintain this trust and am directly accountable to our core stakeholders including our customers, our business partners (from factories to retailers), our employees, our owner Berkshire Hathaway (and its shareholders), and the communities in which we operate. We are creating a framework for when and how to engage in the many issues these stakeholders care about. We communicate regularly to these stakeholders about our brand purpose (inspire you to run your path), initiatives supporting the planet (sustainability), and initiatives supporting people (diversity, equity, and inclusion). As other issues come up, we will assess our standing as a brand to speak and act on them. Then the real challenge will be to follow through for real impact. Mere words will not suffice.

→ Inspiring an Active Lifestyle in the Face of a Public Health Crisis

Brooks's purpose of inspiring everyone to run their path syncs into the role of an active life to stay healthy, which is now more evident than ever as we grapple with the COVID-19 pandemic. Everything good in life starts with being healthy. At Brooks, we singularly focus on the power of the run both as a competitive sport and an investment in your own fitness, health, and wellness. The pandemic crisis highlights the value of stronger efforts to promote a healthier lifestyle to address the comorbidities that have made so many millions more vulnerable to the virus. Good nutrition and an active lifestyle (and yes, that includes running!) are key to avoiding and surviving so many diseases. The obesity and inactivity epidemic has grown tremendously over the past thirty years. New habits for a more active lifestyle will both increase resistance to disease and reduce health care costs.

As I write this, we are still in the throes of a global pandemic and nearly two years in, the impact has been stunning. While many of us have access to the best health care in the world—and in the United States we spend 18 percent of the gross domestic product (GDP) to get it—our public health system was utterly blindsided by a novel virus and ill equipped to handle it. Michael Lewis chronicles many of those shortcomings in his book, *The Premonition: A Pandemic Story*. The global pandemic was our first in more than a hundred years; in hindsight we were clearly unprepared for it. We lacked coherent leadership to defend against a highly transmissible, potentially lethal, and evolving virus. As recently as 2018, the White House disbanded the Directorate of Global Health Security and Biodefense. We were all individually and collectively exposed and at risk.

As of May 2021, there were more than 3.5 million official deaths recorded globally due to COVID-19. However, a study by the Institute for Health Metrics and Evaluation (IHME, an independent global health research center at the University of Washington) estimates that those deaths actually exceed seven million. Some of us let precautions like masks become political statements, which is sad, divisive, and needlessly risky. The cost of this virus on health is tragic but add to that the economic disruption now in the trillions of dollars and it is on the scale of World War II. Let that sink in: *Trillions!*

In the face of this crisis, a science-based approach to the virus created vaccines in less than one year that are more than 90 percent effective and are now being manufactured and delivered at unprecedented scale. This speedy, highly effective innovation has changed life for millions globally as vaccines are rolled out. This is a prime example of America at its best: innovation driven by entrepreneurs, biopharmaceutical companies, and yes, the federal government, which sponsored vital research through the National Institutes of Health (NIH) and public-private sector coordination through Operation Warp Speed. We should insist our federal government make the necessary hundred-year investments (sums only a government can make) to prepare us for the next one. By saving potentially millions of lives and trillions in economic burden, the ROI (return on investment) on a few billion dollars of public health preparedness is outstanding. We will all be better off if more people are active and healthy, and if our public health institutions are more prepared for the next highly transmissible virus.

→ Protecting the Planet We Run On in the Face of Climate Change

Global climate change has now been widely recognized as one of the biggest threats to life, economic health, and societal stability that we face, if not *the* biggest. Once again, I think it is an issue that every business will have to engage in as customers, employees, communities, and increasingly investors will want to know more about a business's impact on climate change. Organizations including the International Monetary Fund, the United Nations, and the U.S. Department of Defense have all made it a priority focus driven by extensive science-based evidence. While any one person or company might choose not to worry about it, collectively we have no choice but to address it with action. After all, every species and more than 7.5 billion people's lives and economic livelihoods depend on a stable environment.

It is clear to us at Brooks that runners are uniquely aware of the necessity of addressing climate change. Because 150 million (and counting) people run outside today (including us), it's critical we take care of the planet we share. At Brooks, we believe in a world where everyone is welcome to run and has a place to do it. We champion the run while we work to reduce the environmental impact of our business operations. We are committed to a long-term, science-backed approach to sustainability and so we've signed the Climate Pledge to achieve net-zero carbon emissions by 2040. To get there, we committed to implement initiatives and innovations including efficiency improvements, renewable energy, materials reductions, and other carbon emission elimination strategies. We also are focused on sustainable consumption, which includes the transition to recycled or renewable materials and the elimination of waste to landfills, leading to the first fully circular performance running footwear and apparel by 2030. Beginning in 2021, Brooks made its number one selling product, the Ghost, carbon neutral through a combination of recycled materials and high-quality carbon offsets.

We've committed to a sustainable supply chain and fair labor practices. All of Brooks's products and materials will be sourced from manufacturing facilities that comply with our Supplier Code of Conduct and Responsible Sourcing Standards designed to protect workers and the environment. We can't solve for the planet on our own, but our 2040 carbon neutral commitment drives our team to do our part.

→ Championing the Run for All— The Inclusion Imperative

A true reckoning on racism in America took center stage with the senseless murder of George Floyd by a Minneapolis police officer on May 25, 2020. It was the latest in a long list of incidents where unarmed Black people died at the hands of law enforcement. Earlier in the year, the shooting of Ahmaud Arbery, a Black man who was jogging in a Georgia neighborhood, shocked us at Brooks and strengthened our resolve to engage and act. While many look across society and see progress since the 1964 Civil Rights Act and the 1965 Voting Rights Act, so much more is needed in this country to address systemic issues in education, justice, access, and opportunity not to mention hatred and violence.

At Brooks, we believe everyone deserves to run on equal ground, and that begins inside the company. We've set measurable goals to build a diverse, equitable, and inclusive workplace and are making progress against them. We are committed to have our team reflect our customer base with 30 percent Black, indigenous, and other people of color (BIPOC) and 50 percent women representation among US Brooks employees at every level. We will maintain our Human Rights Campaign "Corporate Equality Index" score of 100 and support and celebrate the LGBTQ+ communities in running. We welcome and engage diverse runners at a brand level through product development, consumer research, ambassador/athlete programs, and brand marketing campaigns. We are active in partnerships that lift communities and invite more people to put one foot in front of the other. With Dick's Sporting Goods we offer special footwear and apparel through the "Empower Her" collection that benefits girls' running programs in underserved communities nationwide. We are proud to be a founding partner of the Running Industry Diversity Coalition (RIDC). The coalition brings together running brands, running retailers, and BIPOC runners who are working to increase diversity within the sport of running and the industry.

We believe that creating a more inclusive sport and industry is in our sights, but creating a more just society with equal opportunities for all will require broader change. Good governance in business includes having an organization that reflects the diversity of your customer base and your community. At Brooks, we benchmark against the US population as a proxy for the running community. For good governance in a democratic nation, elected officials need to reflect the will and diversity of their citizens, or trust will evaporate. In our democracy, that will is powered by people's right to vote and the access to do so. In America right now, trust in the system is at risk of crumbling when state laws blatantly or even subtly suppress the votes of minority citizens. The goal should be to make voting easy and more accessible, yet in dozens of states the opposite is happening. This is indefensible given the history of voter suppression efforts targeting the Black community and the need to build trust and accountability for our country's future. In 2020, Brooks made Election Day a paid holiday to encourage and enable every employee to vote and volunteer in efforts to create voting access for others.

→ Strengthening Our Economy by Addressing Income Inequality

Brooks is a branded products business that is committed to inspiring and welcoming all into running and an active lifestyle, but we know the income of our customer matters. The truth is that the choice to invest in your health and fitness and take up running requires you to first satisfy life's basic needs. If you are struggling to feed or care for yourself or your family and are working two or more jobs to make ends meet, taking time to be active will often fall by the wayside. For Brooks, the stronger the middle class, the more people who will have the time and wherewithal to invest in their fitness.

Income inequality is also a driver of sports participation and the public health risk factor. A May 2021 report from the Aspen Institute found that wealthier children played sports more during the pandemic than poorer kids. As I said earlier, everything good in life starts with being healthy. Activity matters for everyone, and the gaps are evident between the rich and the poor in health, education, and economic opportunities. It turns out our income inequality is also highly correlated with both inactivity and obesity, which are key risks driving health care costs in our system. Though Brooks cannot solve income inequality on a broad-based, systemic level, we can help provide access to running in communities that are disproportionality affected by income inequality. One of the programs I'm most proud of at Brooks is our Brooks Booster Club, a needs-based grant program that provides performance running footwear, apparel, and funding to under-resourced high school cross country and track teams. Since 2015, the Brooks Booster Club has granted 150 schools and 6,100 runners nationwide, investing more than $2.1 million in cash and gear to keep these programs alive.

From a young age, I was awed by and became infatuated with the potential, promise, and yes, the "specialness" of the evolving American experiment as a liberal democracy:

- a government representative of the people with fair elections of leaders,
- a separation of powers into different branches of government,
- the rule of law in everyday life as part of an open society,
- a market economy with private property, and

- the equal protection of human rights, civil rights, civil liberties, and religious and political freedoms for all people.

But with decades of most of the economic benefits flowing to the top 1 percent, many people now sense that the economy and the system is not working for them, and the data is clear: They are right (see figures 16 and 17).

Since March 2020, the Federal Reserve has injected more than $4 trillion into the economy through the purchase of treasury, bank, and private debt securities resulting in many companies getting financed through the economic crisis than otherwise would be the case. Couple that with $2.8 trillion in federal government support to individuals and businesses, and the scale of the nearly $7 trillion in support and stimulus is hard to fathom. The wealthiest 1 percent and businesses with strong balance sheets and profits were strong coming into the crisis following nearly a decade of economic growth, rising

The gaps in income between upper-income and middle- and lower-income households are rising, and the share held by middle-income households is falling

Median household income, in 2018 dollars, and share of U.S. aggregate household income, by income tier

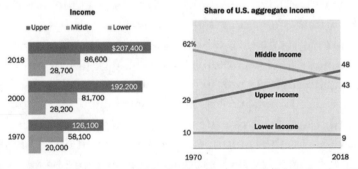

Note: Households are assigned to income tiers based on their size-adjusted income. Incomes are scaled to reflect a three-person household. Revisions to the Current Population Survey affect the comparison of income data from 2014 onwards. See Methodology for details.
Source: Pew Research Center analysis of the Current Population Survey, Annual Social and Economic Supplements (IPUMS).
"Most Americans Say There Is Too Much Economic Inequality in the U.S., but Fewer Than Half Call It a Top Priority"

PEW RESEARCH CENTER

Figure 16

U.S. has highest level of income inequality among G7 countries

Gini coefficient of gross income inequality, latest year available

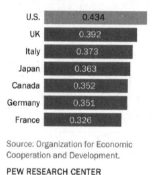

U.S.	0.434
UK	0.392
Italy	0.373
Japan	0.363
Canada	0.352
Germany	0.351
France	0.326

Source: Organization for Economic Cooperation and Development.

PEW RESEARCH CENTER

Figure 17

equity and real estate valuations plus major tax cuts in 2018. After the stimulus, the world is now awash in capital as evidenced by a rebounding stock market, increasing asset values from real estate to commodities. The net of all of this is that wealth is accelerating in this new decade for those who have it while making everything more expensive for those who do not.

Another driver of inequality over the last forty years has been industry consolidation as there are fewer competitive companies in every industry. Structurally, we need to address antitrust laws and enforcement. Or better stated, we need to create new competition laws that address the consolidation across our economy. I have some experience on this topic as I wrote economic analysis for merger approval submissions to regulatory authorities at Pillsbury. At Tuck, one of my favorite classes featured Judge Robert Bork's influential book *The Antitrust Paradox*. A lasting influence of the book was that the principal criteria that should be used for antitrust policy is consumer benefit. This philosophy changed policy in the government and the courts, allowing rampant consolidation leading to many monopolies, near monopolies, and cartel-like industry structures causing much destruction of smaller businesses across the landscape. In economics and life, a singular focus on one thing such as consumer benefit can be taken too far and create other problems including decimating whole industries, competition, and jobs. It is time to go back to more balanced policies incorporating the impact on competition in the industries. New voices including Senator Amy Klobuchar in her recent book *Antitrust: Taking on Monopoly Power from the Gilded Age to the Digital Age* are leading the path forward. The impact of less concentrated industries over time would be more companies competing, innovating, and creating jobs across the economy.

Finally, a myriad of other policies have contributed to our nation's economic gains disproportionally benefiting the top 1 percent. These include the impact of globalization on jobs, the decline of unions, the lack of a living minimum wage, compelling training and apprentice opportunities in the trades, the cost and access to education (and the resulting student loan burdens), lack of affordable childcare, lack of early learning for children, and a fair-share tax system. The tax disparities have compounded over decades and not only starve us from making health care, housing, infrastructure, and education accessible to all, but accelerate wealth for those who already have it. If the specialness of the American idea and the engine of capitalism doesn't benefit all, people will lose trust in it. Again, our economy is not a zero-sum game, there is enough wealth created for everyone to be better off.

This is a big list but for me it is akin to my "wall of bricks" analogy on driving critical business priorities forward in support of a greater mission. I believe with hope restored to people of an on-ramp to opportunities, a better life for them and their children, and a broader middle class, we will have a stronger economy that offers more and better-paying jobs. At Brooks we have been fortunate that the running category is large, global, competitive, and not owned or consolidated by one brand or retailer. If other industries were less consolidated, there would be more challenger brand stories like Brooks, which would give consumers more choices and drive economic vitality across more communities.

→ Be Part of Something Bigger Than Yourself

Born in 1960, I inherited values from the Greatest Generation that drove me to be part of something important; to lean in and hook my wagon to a leader, a cause, an idea bigger than myself. I learned at a young age that the highest calling was not just to score goals. The team comes first. USA Hockey coach Herb Brooks put it well when talking about a player's hockey jersey in the film *Miracle on Ice:* "The name on the front is a hell of a lot more important than the one on the back." As a leader, I have always seen the goal as winning but not at other people's expense.

While competitive sport is often a zero-sum game, life and business are not. There are lots of ways to succeed if the rules are respected and equally applied. Author and investor Jacqueline Novogratz describes the opposite of poverty as not income but dignity. Imagine a world in which everyone in society sees hope, feels dignity, and believes that the game is fair with broad-based opportunities for all. The white space for trust would be filled. It is both a challenge and an opportunity, and I am committed to do my part as I play my role in the business, brand, and team at Brooks.

CHAPTER 11

On Your Left! Running Fast in a New Decade

CONSIDER MYSELF FORTUNATE ON SO MANY LEVELS for the opportunities I continue to have. Brooks has not only survived the economic disruption of the pandemic but has emerged stronger, poised to successfully compete for the affinity of runners. As you know by now, I am in the job I have wanted since seventh grade: running a successful business with dedicated people who work hard and creatively every day to deliver on our goals. A business with a higher purpose that is on a mission to build a great, trustable brand. A business offering products and experiences that improve people's lives. I pinch myself every day because I have the best job in the business world.

Berkshire expects us to run our business as if we own it, but for me, the often-unspoken expectations are to play at a high level and maximize the value, ROI, cash flow, and potential of their investment. Because we all know that success will come from a great brand, we are obsessed with runners and know that our execution for them will always come from our people.

So, I get to be a leader and play the role of chief of strategy, culture, brand, risk, and executive officer for a running brand. Insert Smiley Face! I am "running down a dream" and have never been more excited or optimistic about Brooks's opportunities to build a distinctive, global brand in the amazing sport and fitness space of running.

At Brooks, we are running with purpose.

→ The Power of the Run Is Alive and Well

The best decision we ever made at Brooks was to focus on the sport and fitness lifestyle of running. Competitive track and field, cross country, road racing, endurance, and trail races now all represent the sport of running. If you have yet to join one of your local 5K events, I highly recommend it. Being at the start of a race and hanging out at the finish line has always been inspiring to me no matter the distance. The energy of the people is universally positive as they toe-up to the line and push themselves to compete. Millions more come out to local races to add an event to their running regimen that is an investment in their own fitness. All will be joining a like-minded group of people to run, walk, or move. Many will bring along their friends or families and often raise money for a worthy cause along the way. Running will make their day better.

When the pandemic began to spread across the world in early 2020, like everything else, there was no certainty on how it would affect our customers from retailers to runners. We thought running might make the cut in people's lives as a convenient, outdoor, social-distance friendly activity that delivers on so many levels for both physical and mental health. With the competitive sport shut down from the middle school level through the Olympics, it was the solo fitness runner who took charge. Now with the sport and events returning, we believe running will be sticky for so many who picked it up during the pandemic. We are now in a new running boom with more than 150 million people running worldwide and a $33 billion market.

In those dark days of spring 2020, it did remind me of *The Grinch Who Stole Christmas*. The joyful climax of the story occurs when all of the Whos down in Whoville stroll out singing on Christmas morning despite the fact there are no longer decorations, trees, gifts, or feasts on the table. The lesson is clear: the spirit of Christmas endures regardless of the Grinch's evil efforts. I thought of Dr. Seuss's parable as the pandemic began to ease. COVID-19 was like the Grinch and all of us in the running community were the Whos in Whoville. Even the ravages of a global pandemic could not steal the spirit of running. We all knew that running was a meaningful way to stay healthy in the face of a deadly virus. The power of running in people's lives is what prevailed. The run was just out your front door.

The spectacle that is track and field, the marathon, or an epic endurance race remains the center of gravity for our sport and inspires millions to lace up and enter a race on the roads. Getting outside for fresh air and experiencing forests, hills, lakes, and beautiful places is drawing millions more to hike, run, and race on the trails and in the mountains. Finally, millions have come to appreciate the treadmill! It has always been a convenient and safe way to get in miles, but during the pandemic it saw a resurgence in use. In this decade there will be more ways than ever to run and stay connected to others physically and digitally along your path.

As we look ahead at Brooks, we believe the number of people who run could double to more than 300 million people by 2030. First, we see the market being driven by continued global economic growth, technology-enabled productivity gains, a shorter workweek, and broad-based household income growth.

An increased awareness of personal health is driving more people to find the time to invest in being active. This awareness can lead to many more people committing to weekly movement; running will be the activity of choice (second to walking) as a broad-based, iconic, youthful, aerobic, approachable, and accessible sport. We will challenge ourselves at Brooks to be one of the main drivers of the democratization of the run, facilitating access to the sport to all communities, everywhere on the planet.

→ The Brooks Brand Is Setting the Pace

Brooks's Run Happy mantra has always been about celebrating *your* run. No matter how far or how fast. Whether it is your first run, a personal best, an epic rave run in a beautiful place, or winning the Boston Marathon, we celebrate your achievement and your experience. For almost twenty years our stated purpose has been to inspire everyone to run their path. Its power comes from the truth of what running can do for you. If you get your run in today, you will likely be a better, more effective, and maybe even happier person. If you add up a lot of days, it has the chance to make your life better. And if millions of people live that way, the world will be a better place. At Brooks, we are 100 percent focused on engaging with all who run and frankly anyone who puts one foot in front of another. Yes, in our view, walking counts! At my stage in life, I often refer to walking as slow running.

We now believe that no brand will ever "own" running or the runner. It is big and diverse and people run locally. Running is decidedly not a virtual or digital experience but uniquely a human and often social one. As we have built our strategies, our culture, and our team to compete for runners, we have moved up in the industry pack of competitors. We challenge ourselves to create the best gear, tools, and experiences for runners. We compete every day to earn their trust and affinity to be their number-one brand choice. We know that over the next decade, every active and fashion footwear and apparel company will produce run-inspired athleisure product, plus all athletic, outdoor, and fitness brands will create gear to compete for enthusiasts and new runners. The customer will have more great brands and products to choose from.

The onus will be on brands like Brooks to create better and more innovative solutions. I liken the business puzzle to the age-old "content" versus "distribution" debate now raging on screen led by Netflix. Because we believe owning the distribution pipes is not the be-all and end-all for the broad running market, Brooks will operate more like a highly focused "content" company for runners. I believe that in the end, content does win, especially for niche players. It also means that at Brooks, we are firmly committed to a multichannel distribution strategy to be where runners shop for great gear. We think this is the winning strategy in the long term if your goal is to reach runners. Many brands will create a great niche business with a consumer-direct, closed ecosystem. We just don't believe that strategy will prevail to lead with runners.

Brooks's momentum in this new decade is surging with the brand setting all-time records for revenue and growth. Coming off of 27 percent growth in 2020, momentum has accelerated, driven by new runner participation and market share gains. In May 2021, on a twelve-month rolling year basis, Brooks became a $1 billion brand. It is a significant achievement as there are only a few dozen billion-dollar brands in sports and fitness industries.

Brooks is setting the pace with runners by nearly every market metric we track. With a 15 percent share, we are now the number-two brand among runners buying footwear, up 4.8 points in the US market. Brooks remains the leader in performance run footwear in key retail channels including specialty running (26.1 percent share), sporting goods (e.g., Dick's Sporting Goods), and online (e.g., Zappos).

The real value of this growth is in the resulting ability to continue to invest in our brand and people. Brooks's focus on delivering premium performance running products at acceptable margins means we can continue to invest at a scale equal to our largest competitors. We are accelerating investments in product, consumer insights, research and development, systems, supply chain, retail relationships, digital marketing, and runner engagement. Now if we can execute with our people against the opportunity, we absolutely have a chance of winning the runner's trust as their authentic brand choice.

Now in the twentieth year of our focus on the runner, we are beginning to hit our stride as a brand and can articulate to our team members and partners just who we are. As of 2021, this is Brooks (figure 18):

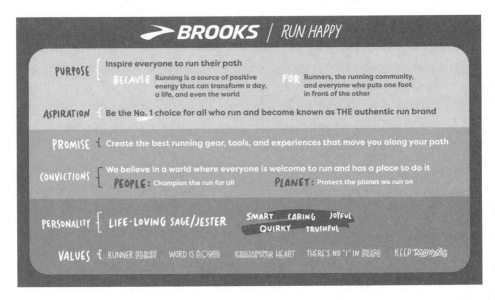

Figure 18

→ Innovation Will Be Essential to Win with Runners

Like so many areas of life, the essence of what we are focused on at Brooks is pretty simple. Even Dr. Anthony Fauci, a runner himself, opined on the challenges of the vaccine rollout in 2021: "It's not like making shoes." While making a perfect running shoe for the individual runner's needs might not be as difficult as creating a new vaccine, our industry finds it far from easy, and the market is full of mediocre shoes. We strive to build great running gear—the world's *best* running gear—and then endeavor to engage with runners in an authentic and relevant way to be their brand of choice. In practice, the bar is high and getting higher. One of the great paradoxes of our industry is that first, runners have a clear idea of what gear they love; they become passionately loyal and opinionated about it, especially their shoe or their run bra. And yet, they crave innovation and are always curious about whether something better is out there. So, at Brooks we continue to try to deliver both consistent product fit and feel, season to season, while also bringing new technology to improve the running experience for your next mile.

What's to come in the next decade for Brooks? Innovation that is science- and runner-driven. Our Run Sights Lab team of talented researchers gather and interpret insights and signals daily through engagement with hundreds of runners from all over the world. Understanding what they need and want consciously and unconsciously is the mission. These learnings, now incorporated in all of our product strategies and briefs, have the potential to turn into innovation when meshed with biomechanical research, design, engineered materials, and new processes. Some of the areas we are most enthusiastic about on the road ahead include:

Tuned ride—footwear using new engineered foams to optimize cushioning, energy return, and support. Brooks recently launched DNA Loft v3 DNA Flash featuring nitrogen-infused compounds, making shoes dramatically lighter and springier, stride after stride.

Additive manufacturing—building shoes through 3D printing based on designs that reflect the runner's needs and preferences biomechanically and anatomically (fit) in a design of their choosing.

Adaptable materials—engineered fibers, materials, and designs that offer fit, control, and comfort based on the runner's body and foot in motion. We are architecting support into run bra fabrics without compromising comfort, breathability, or light weight and partnering with companies like 3M to enhance visibility.

Enhanced running experiences owing to digitization—collecting and curating data from runners (such as running history, injury history, run experience, desires and goals, demographics, and biometrics) with the intention of creating services that will improve their running experiences in real time (for example, better product designs, better shoe selection guidance, and run coaching). The goal for Brooks will be to deliver personal advice based on their data, hand in hand with a one-to-one dialogue. We will know we are hitting the mark when the feedback is: "Brooks understands me best, I love that brand."

With our Planet and People commitments, we also believe that *how* we operate as a company will matter more than ever to our customers. We are committed to innovation in our manufacturing and operations. We will begin to test product circularity by building new shoes from manufacturing waste and from previously worn Brooks shoes by 2025. We are aggressively assessing and implementing low carbon/low waste materials and processes with the goal of getting to 100 percent of our inputs from recycled and renewable materials and sending nothing to landfill. We are creating plans to work with our major footwear factory partners to switch to 100 percent renewable energy at our operating facilities by 2030.

We also believe that a big part of meeting our sustainability goals and getting the best shoe to the runner as fast as they want it will be getting our production closer to market. By 2030, we hope to be manufacturing shoes in all major regions. This will shorten our supply chains, lower shipping costs, and reduce our carbon footprint. Innovations including new lean processes, automated systems, robotics, and 3D printing will be necessary.

It is a given that runners will have more innovation and choice coming to them in the next decade than ever before. That's exciting. It is a sign of a healthy industry. We are running fast to win the race for new runners. On your left!

→ Leadership in the Next Decade: Authenticity Required

These are not easy times to be a leader at any level, whether for a team, a company, a nonprofit organization, a school, a city, or a police department, let alone a state or a national government. I have tried to make the case that now more than ever, there is unaddressed white space for both trust *and* authentic leadership. This seems like a great place to reiterate the principles I have found central to being an effective leader in business. I hope there is some wisdom in them for you:

1. **Own a Niche:** Pursue greatness by simultaneously owning a niche, growing, and delivering premium profits, consistently and over time.

2. **Build a Moat:** Create a distinctive, defendable brand proposition. Getting credit for it from the customer (at full price) is the measure of its strength and essential to sustainable success.

3. **Solve for Profitability:** Engineer it into your business model. If successful, it can create a flywheel of investment to strengthen your moat.

4. **Vision without Execution Is Hallucination:** Dreams and plans are meaningless if they're not backed by action. Walk the talk.

5. **Lead Authentically:** Focus, curiosity, and trust are foundational to connecting with people. Treat them with respect, integrity, and humility.

6. **The Ultimate Advantage Is a Strong Culture.**

CONCLUSION

Life's Short, Run Long

When I began to put the finishing touches on this book in the precious warmer, longer Seattle summer days of 2021, there was much to be hopeful about. Vaccinations were rising worldwide, businesses were reopening, schools were welcoming students back into their buildings, and footraces were resuming. I saw people out running everywhere, often with friends. Some were taking their first run, others participating in their first 5K or 10K. The Angel City Elite track club, dedicated to increasing BIPOC representation in the running community, got its start in Los Angeles with a little help from Brooks. Track fans watched with excitement the fast competition at the Olympic games in Tokyo, albeit one year late due to pandemic delays. At Brooks we cheered on Josh Kerr as he won the bronze medal in the 1500-meter. This followed the record he set earlier in the summer for the fastest 1500-meter ever run on American soil. A member of the Brooks Beasts Track Club, coached by Danny Mackey, Josh set his record at the Stumptown Twilight meet on the campus of Lewis & Clark College in Portland, Oregon. On the same Brooks Beasts team, Nia Akins was runner-up in the women's 800-meter. The bright spotlight of racing stretched around the world. In France, the Meeting de Montreuil returned. In Nashville, the Music City Track Carnival rose again. Australians tapered their training for their marathon championships in Queensland. The runners in Whoville were running.

What binds runners together is the truth in what running does for each of us. It improves the day both for you and those around you. I believe that in business and in life, forward motion is key. Your pace will vary depending on conditions and life events, but momentum is a powerful force and can help pull you through headwinds. I try to find a way to move every day and, better yet, be present for it and soak it in. Running is a gift from me to me. Left foot, right foot, left foot, right foot . . .

In April 2007, a Brooks employee named Liz Duncan set out early one Saturday morning for a group run. A fount of positive energy and optimism, she was training for a sub-3:00 marathon. As she waited on a Seattle street corner for fellow runners to arrive, an out-of-control car jumped the curb, struck her, and killed her on impact. She was three days shy of her twenty-seventh birthday. The following Monday and for quite some time thereafter, it was impossible to walk by Liz's desk and not feel her absence. Her workstation displayed photos of family, friends, and teens she mentored through Athletes in Action. And in the middle of all those smiling faces was her favorite Brooks bumper sticker. It simply said, "Life's short. Run long." Liz used sports to bring people together, to build relationships, character, and hope. Her legacy includes reminding us that life is indeed short, and so we best embrace and make the most of it.

Enthusiasm and optimism are magnetic, and joy is kinetic. Most people appreciate the energy and attitude of a positive, happy, can-do person. As a leader, family member, friend, and citizen, that is what I try to be for others most days and when I am at my best.

Finally, now is the time, more than ever, to *Run with Purpose*. Pick a path, commit, and work every day to make a difference. It can indeed be destiny as articulated so well: "The secret to success is constancy of purpose."

ACKNOWLEDGMENTS

I have come to deeply appreciate people who are really good at what they do. Thousands of hours plus talent, skill, and focus create professionals and experts in every field of play—including writing. I am humbled by great writing, and I knew I would need help on my first book as a rookie author. I have many people to thank who helped me create *Running with Purpose.*

The manuscript came together under the guidance of Greg Shaw of Clyde Hill Publishing who became a key partner in curating and sorting stories from decades of documents and experiences for both Brooks and me. I found Greg networking in Seattle and with our New York agency partners, and as a lifelong runner, he was the perfect partner for the book. Greg crafted the outline and helped me to structure and integrate the best stories from start to finish.

Tamara Hills was also a key editor on the book from beginning to end just as she has been for over eleven years as my chief of staff at Brooks where we cocreate and edit much of the communication that comes from my office. Tamara is in many ways an embodiment of the Brooks brand and culture and was a pivotal partner to capture, curate, and edit stories and milestones on the Brooks journey.

Greg Shaw introduced me to the legendary Jim Levine at Levine Greenberg Rostan Literary Agency who graciously took me on as a client and found Sara Kendrick at HarperCollins Leadership to publish the book. The editors at HarperCollins Leadership including Linda Alila and Louis Greenstein took my rough manuscript and expertly polished it.

This story would not exist if not for the people of Brooks, both past and present, for leaning in to write our own script to build a brand and a company through hard work and champion heart. It has been the honor and joy of my life to be on the same team with each of them. Specific to the storytelling within the book and our efforts to share the work with others, I am grateful for the input, support, and feedback from Dan Sheridan, Patrick Pons de Vier, Melanie Allen, Tom Ross, Katie Carlson, Barbara Barrilleaux, Mark Koppes, Rick Wilhelm, Carson Caprara, Pete Humphrey, Alaina Fuld, Jess Lyons, and members of Brooks's Creative and Legal teams.

The support from Berkshire Hathaway has been rock solid at every moment of the Brooks journey, and I appreciate the encouragement from Warren Buffett and Greg Abel on this book. In Brooks's early days, the courage, fortitude, patience, and capital from the partners of J.H. Whitney Capital created the foundation for this great story, and I will always be grateful to Brooks Board Chair Ann Iverson and Whitney partners Paul Vigano and Peter Castleman for giving me the keys to drive this car.

Charlotte Guyman, a longtime board member to both Brooks and Berkshire Hathaway, was generous with her time and depth of knowledge of all things Brooks to give the manuscript a careful read and make many thoughtful suggestions on areas to amplify. Former Brooks board member and friend Robbie Bach also gifted his time, asking insightful, clarifying questions and offering helpful guidance to sharpen key messages.

Two key professionals helped me express my insights and convictions on leadership in these times when business is being asked to speak and act for change. I am grateful to Cheryl Overton, the Founder of Cheryl Overton Communications, LLC, for her insightful and direct guidance on speaking authentically. Harvey Floyd II, an organizational psychologist, executive coach, and lecturer at Wharton Executive Education, brought perspective, wisdom, and context while challenging me to articulate strong convictions.

I want to give a collective and spirited shout-out to all of the teachers, coaches, teammates, athletes, professors, bosses, co-workers, board members, my brothers and sisters, and friends who taught, challenged, counseled, guided, and often showed me by example a path to finding who I am and where I could make a positive difference in this world.

Finally, from the first word to last, I valued the continuous inspiration, love, and support of my wife MaryEllen; my children and their spouses Michael, Kacey, Joel, Marisa, and Reid; and our four grandchildren Teagan, Declan, Lennon, and Esme, who unfailingly create joy in my day.

BIBLIOGRAPHY

Chapter 1

Buffett, Warren E. Chairman's Letter—1984. Berkshire Hathaway. February 25, 1985. https://www.berkshirehathaway.com/letters/1984.html.

Hafer, R. W. "The Prime Rate and the Cost of Funds: Is the Prime Too High?" *Review* (Federal Reserve Bank of St. Louis) 65, no. 5 (May 1983): 17–21. https://files.stlouisfed.org/files/htdocs/publications/review/83/05/PrimeRate_May1983.pdf.

Urquhart, Michael A., and Marilyn A. Hewson. "Unemployment Continued to Rise in 1982 as Recession Deepened." *Monthly Labor Review* 106, no. 2 (February 1983): 3–12. https://www.bls.gov/opub/mlr/1983/02/art1full.pdf.

Chapter 2

Buzzell, Robert D, and Bradley T. Gale. *The PIMS Principles, Profit Impact of Market Strategy-Linking Strategy to Performance.* New York: The Free Press, 1987.

"The Coleman Company, Inc. Company Profile, Information, Business Description, History, Background Information on The Coleman Company, Inc." *Reference for Business Encyclopedia.* https://www.referenceforbusiness.com/history2/78/The-Coleman-Company-Inc.html.

McDowell, Edwin. "Coleman Is Glowing Overseas." *New York Times,* December 9, 1991. https://www.nytimes.com/1991/12/09/business/coleman-is-glowing-overseas.html?.

Cuff, Daniel F. "Grand Met Bids to Buy Pillsbury." *New York Times,* October 4, 1988. https://www.nytimes.com/1988/10/04/business/grand-met-bids-to-buy-pillsbury.html

Hayes, Thomas C. "Pillsbury's Controversial Chief." *New York Times,* August 24, 1984. https://timesmachine.nytimes.com/timesmachine/1981/08/24/244690.html?pageNumber=49

Chapter 3

Boston Athletic Association. "History of the Boston Marathon." https://www.baa.org/races/boston-marathon/history.

Glascock, Stuart. "A Light Step." *Seattle Business,* January 2011. https://www.seattlebusinessmag.com/article/light-step.

Telegraph. "Moment in Time: April 19, 1967 Boston Marathon—Kathrine Switzer Attacked by Official Mid Race." August 24, 1984. https://www.telegraph.co.uk/athletics/2019/04/18/moment-time-april-19-1967-boston-marathon-kathrine-switzer/.

Wilhelm, Steve. "Brooks Sprints to High-End Niche." *Puget Sound Business Journal,* March 11, 2001. https://www.bizjournals.com/seattle/stories/2001/03/12/story5.html

Chapter 4

Weber, Jim. "2019 Carlson School Commencement Keynote Speech." Keynote presented at the University of Minnesota's Carlson School of Management 2019 Commencement ceremonies, Minneapolis, MN, May 21, 2019. https://carlsonschool.umn.edu/node/107296.

Chapter 5

Brooks Sports. *Run Signature: Follow Your Body. Find Your Run.* 2013. https://www.brooksrunning.com/on/demandware.static/-/Sites-BrooksRunning EMEA-Library/default/dwf6542532/SS/RunSignatureEbook.pdf.

Buffett, Warren. "2002 Chairman's Letter." February 21, 2003. https://www.berkshirehathaway.com/letters/2002pdf.pdf

Elite Racing, Inc. "Original Rock 'n' Roll Marathon Begins New Decade in San Diego." Press release, January 24, 2008. https://www.prweb.com/releases/rock_n_roll_marathon/elite_racing/prweb641601.html.

Furrer, Amanda. "A Jack of All Trades, the Brooks Ghost 12 Is Suited for Every Kind of Run." *Runner's World,* September 4, 2019. https://www.runnersworld.com/gear/a28903544/brooks-ghost-12-review/.

Garnick, Coral. "Brooks Sports Running Strong at 100." *Seattle Times,* updated June 20, 2014. https://www.seattletimes.com/business/brooks-sports-running-strong-at-100/.

Hutchinson, Alex. "Footstrike at the Olympic Trials." *Runner's World,* June 25, 2012. https://www.runnersworld.com/training/a20826847 /footstrike-at-the-olympic-trials/.

Jim Collins. "BHAG." https://www.jimcollins.com/concepts/bhag.html.

Larson, Peter. "Is The Minimalist Trend Over?—Comments on Injury Risk and Sales Data." *Runblogger,* June 24, 2013. https://runblogger.com/2013 /06/is-minimalist-trend-over-comments-on.html.

Max, Sarah. "Brooks Sports Moves New Home Closer to Trails." *New York Times,* July 29, 2014. https://www.nytimes.com/2014/07/30/realestate /commercial/brooks-sports-moves-new-home-closer-to-trails.html.

McCue, Matt. "More Than 150,000 Claims Filed in Vibram Class Action Suit." *Runner's World,* November 18, 2014. https://www.runnersworld.com /gear/a20835909/more-than-150-000-claims-filed-in-vibram-class-action -suit/.

McDougall, Christopher. *Born to Run: A Hidden Tribe, Superathletes, and the Greatest Race the World Has Never Seen.* New York: Alfred A. Knopf, 2009.

Metzler, Brian. "20 Things You Probably Didn't Know About Running Shoes." *PodiumRunner,* May 24, 2014. https://www.podiumrunner.com /gear/sole-man-13-things-you-didnt-know-about-running-shoes/.

Newman, Andrew Adam. "Brooks, Maker of Elite Shoes, Takes Aim at the Fun Run Crowd." *New York Times,* June 10, 2010. https://www.nytimes.com /2010/06/11/business/media/11adco.html.

Running Insight. "Brooks Says 'PureProject' Launch Biggest in Its History." April 1, 2011. https://www.mydigitalpublication.com/publication/?i=65821 &view=.

Ryan, Tom. "Brooks Looks to Become Next Billion Dollar Running Brand." *Performance Sports Retailer,* April 2010. https://www.yumpu.com/en /document/read/26527418/hi-res-version-sportsonesourcecom.

Chapter 6

Berkshire Hathaway. *2020 Annual Report,* February 27, 2021. https://www .berkshirehathaway.com/2020ar/2020ar.pdf

Buffett, Warren E. *An Owner's Manual.* Omaha: Berkshire Hathaway, 1996.

Buffett, Warren E. *Berkshire Hathaway 2020 Shareholder Letter.* Berkshire Hathaway, February 27, 2021. https://www.berkshirehathaway.com/letters /2020ltr.pdf.

Cunningham, Lawrence A. *Berkshire Beyond Buffett: The Enduring Value of Values.* New York: Columbia University Press, 2014.

Friedman, Milton. "A Friedman Doctrine—The Social Responsibility of Business Is to Increase Its Profits." *New York Times*, September 13, 1970. https://www.nytimes.com/1970/09/13/archives/a-friedman-doctrine-the -social-responsibility-of-business-is-to.html.

Schwantes, Marcel. "Warren Buffett Says Everyone Has Intelligence and Energy but Without This Success Trait, Forget Everything." *Inc.*, August 6, 2018. https://www.inc.com/marcel-schwantes/warren-buffett-says-everyone -has-intelligence-energy-but-without-this-success-trait-forget-everything.html.

Chapter 7

Bachman, Rachel. "How Millennials Ended the Running Boom." *Wall Street Journal*, May 5, 2016. https://www.wsj.com/articles/how-millennials-ended -the-running-boom-1462473195.

Goldman Sachs. "Millennials Infographic." https://www.goldmansachs.com /insights/archive/millennials.

In the Loop. "Why Under Armour Is Buying Up Fitness Apps." Aired February 5, 2015, on Bloomberg TV. https://www.bloomberg.com/news /videos/2015-02-05/why-under-armour-is-buying-up-fitness-apps.

Rosenfeld, Jill. "CDU to Gretzky: The Puck Stops Here!" *Fast Company*, June 30, 2000. https://www.fastcompany.com/40565/cdu-gretzky-puck -stops-here

Chapter 8

Rocheleau, Matt. "Is this the worst weather ever at the Boston Marathon?" *Boston Globe*, April 16, 2018. https://www.bostonglobe.com/metro/2018 /04/16/this-worst-weather-ever-boston-marathon-took-look-back-most -miserable-years/pfpqsGY3kuS0rwDw5afKyH/story.html.

Chapter 9

Frankl, Victor E. *Man's Search for Meaning*, 4th ed. Boston: Beacon Press, 2000.

Chapter 10

Aspen Institute. *Project Play: COVID-19 Parenting Survey III.* April 2021. https://www.aspeninstitute.org/wp-content/uploads/2021/05/COVID-19 -Parenting-Survey-FINAL-REPORT-v2.pdf.

Bork, Robert H. *The Antitrust Paradox: A Policy at War with Itself.* New York: Basic Books, 1978.

Brooks Staff. "We're proud to sign The Climate Pledge." *Brooks Running* (blog), December 9, 2020. https://www.brooksrunning.com/en_ca/blog /inspiring-stories/the-climate-pledge.html.

Centers for Medicare & Medicaid Services (CMS). "National Health Expenditure Data." December 16, 2020. https://www.cms.gov/Research -Statistics-Data-and-Systems/Statistics-Trends-and-Reports/NationalHealth ExpendData/NationalHealthAccountsHistorical.

Institute for Health Metrics and Evaluation (IHME). *Estimation of Total Mortality Due to COVID-19.* May 13, 2021. http://www.healthdata.org/special -analysis/estimation-excess-mortality-due-covid-19-and-scalars-reported -covid-19-deaths.

International Olympic Committee. "Rio 2016 5000m Men Results." https:// olympics.com/en/olympic-games/rio-2016/results/athletics/5000m-men.

Klobuchar, Amy. *Antitrust: Taking on Monopoly Power from the Gilded Age to the Digital Age.* New York: Alfred A. Knopf, 2021.

Lewis, John. "Bloody Sunday Commemoration." Remarks delivered at Edmund Pettus Bridge, Selma, AL, March 1, 2020.

Lewis, Michael. *The Premonition: A Pandemic Story.* New York: W.W. Norton & Company, 2021.

Muniz-Pardos, Borja, Shaun Sutehall, Konstantinos Angeloudis, Fergus M. Guppy, Andrew Bosch, and Yannis Pitsiladis. "Recent Improvements in Marathon Run Times Are Likely Technological, Not Physiological." *Sports Medicine* 51, no. 3 (March 1, 2021): 371–78. https://doi.org/10.1007 /s40279-020-01420-7.

Novogratz, Jacqueline. "The Opposite of Poverty." *Medium,* April 25, 2016. https://acumenideas.com/the-opposite-of-poverty-8534d6fa7102.

Pew Research Center. "The Gaps in Income between Upper-Income and Middle- and Lower-Income Households Are Rising, and the Share Held by Middle-Income Households Is Falling." February 7, 2020. https://www .pewresearch.org/fact-tank/2020/02/07/6-facts-about-economic-inequality -in-the-u-s/ft_2020-02-07_inequality_06/.

Pew Research Center. "U.S. Has Highest Level of Income Inequality Among G7 Countries." February 7, 2020. https://www.pewresearch.org/fact-tank /2020/02/07/6-facts-about-economic-inequality-in-the-u-s/ft_20-02-04 _economicinequality_2/.

Stern, Steven Hilliard, dir. *Miracle on Ice*. New York, NY: American Broadcasting Company, 1981.

Washington Post. "Relative Growth of After-Tax-and-Transfer Income." December 9, 2019. https://www.washingtonpost.com/opinions/2019/12 /09/massive-triumph-rich-illustrated-by-stunning-new-data/.

Weber, Jim. "2019 Carlson School Commencement Keynote Speech." Keynote presented at the University of Minnesota's Carlson School of Management 2019 Commencement ceremonies, Minneapolis, MN, May 21, 2019. https://carlsonschool.umn.edu/node/107296.

Chapter 11

Arnsdorf, Isaac, and Ryan Gabrielson. "Why We Can't Make Vaccine Doses Any Faster." *ProPublica*, February 19, 2021. https://www.propublica.org /article/covid-vaccine-supply.

Brooks Sports. "Brooks Running Gains New Runners with 49% Global Growth in Q3." November 18, 2020. https://www.brooksrunning.com/en _us/11-18-2020/.

Moreton, Jacob. "Josh Kerr Beats Seb Coe's 1500m US Record." *Runner's World*, June 11, 2021. https://www.runnersworld.com/uk/news/a36696156 /josh-kerr-beats-seb-coes-1500m-us-record/.

INDEX

Page numbers followed by *f* indicate figures, charts, or graphs. *Italic* page numbers indicate photographs.

ABCs of business decay, 70, 122
Abel, Greg, 118, 119, 158, 161
accountability:
    at Berkshire, 122
    at Coleman, 31–32
active lifestyle, public health and, 182–184
adaptable materials, 200
Addiction (Brooks shoe), 53, 77
additive manufacturing, 200
Adidas, 42, 43, 129
Adrenaline GTS (Brooks shoe):
    and barefoot running earthquake, 77
    redesign of, 64–65
    reinvention as GTS 4, 53–54
    as statement product, 60
    success of, 58, 73
    Mark Zuckerberg and, 115
Adrenaline GTS 4 (Brooks shoe), 53–54, 65
Akins, Nia, 203
Albertson, Clayton "CJ," 157
Albrecht, Judy, 48
alignment, culture and, 144–147
Allen, Melanie, 135–136
Amazon.com, 134–135
Angel City Elite track club, 203
Antitrust (Klobuchar), 191
The Antitrust Paradox (Bork), 190
Arbery, Ahmaud, 161, 186
Armstrong, Lance, 180

Asics, 30, 42, 43, 60, 98
Asics 2000 series shoe, 64
athleisure footwear, 45
Athletes in Action, 204
authenticity, 59–72
    and Brooks's brand positioning, 94–96, 145
    as core of successful leadership, 65–69
    defining a North Star for, 61–65
    essence of, 69–72
    genesis of authentic brands, 60
    and leadership in 2020s, 201–202

Bach, Robbie, 120
"barbecue" shoes, 45
barefoot running, 75–79
Barefoot Ted, 76
Beast (Brooks shoe), 53, 58, 77
Berkshire Hathaway:
    acquisition of Russell Athletic, 57
    assistance to Brooks during COVID pandemic, 158
    Brooks as stand-alone subsidiary of, 101, 115–118
    business model of, 105–106
    corporate governance, 118–120
    and Cowles Media, 19–20
    lessons for Brooks, 121–124
    proposal to make Brooks a direct subsidiary of, 106
    unspoken expectations for Brooks, 192–193
Berkshire Hathaway Board of Directors, 115–118
Berkshire Hathaway "Invest in Yourself" 5K race, 117–118

Berkshire Hathaway Shoe (Brooks limited edition shoe), 113
Berlin Marathon (2008), 73
Big 5 Sporting Goods, 42, 47–48, 51
Big Endorsement Campaign, 133
Big Hairy Audacious Goal (BHAG), 78
Biwott, Shadrack, 147, 150
Boeing, 180
Bohan, David, 52
Bork, Robert, 190
Born to Run (McDougall), 75–76, 80
Boston Marathon, 43, *44,* 147–150
Boulder Running Company, 78
Boys State, 109–110
brand positioning, 63, 79, 94–96, 94*f,* 95*f* (*see also* Run Happy)
brand values, 140*f*
Bridle Trails State Park (King County, Washington), 14
Brooks, Herb, 192
Brooks Advisory Board, 119–120
Brooks Beasts Track Club, 203
Brooks Blue, 47
Brooks Booster Club, 188
Brooks Cavalcade of Curiosities, 90–91
Brooks Gurus, 154, 160
Brooks Heritage line, 131
Brooks Running:
    100th anniversary celebration, 100–101
    acquisition by Russell Athletic, 57–58
    becoming an authentic leader, 59–72
    Berkshire's lessons for, 121–124
    brand values, 140*f*
    defining a North Star, 61–65
    distribution choices, 47–50
    forming a personal leadership manifesto at, 38–40
    global revenue 2008–2014, 98
    global sales meeting (May 2016), 132–133

    innovation in 2020s, 199–201
    international distributors' meeting (2001), 42–45
    J.H. Whitney and, 112
    one-page strategy, 64*f*
    revenue and growth in 2020s, 197–198
    and Rock 'n' Roll Marathon, 90
    rolling 12-month revenue trend (2014–2020), 162*f*
    scaling for growth, 151–156
    shifting of sole focus to running, 41–58
    Jim Weber's acceptance of presidency position, 40
    and Weber's experiences at Tuck, 21–22
    Whitney's acquisition of, 37–38
Bryant, Kobe, 57
Buffalo Evening News, 19–20
Buffett, Warren, 101
    and Berkshire Hathaway's acquisition of Russell, 58
    and Berkshire "Invest in Yourself" 5K race, 117–118
    and brands, 39
    at Brooks, 120–121
    on CDOs, 75
    and Cowles Media, 19–20
    importance of passionate employees, 122
    Omaha meeting with Jim Weber, 113–115
    proposal to make Brooks a direct subsidiary of Berkshire Hathaway, 106
    Jim Weber and, 105–106
    and Jim Weber's cancer and, 169, 173
    and Jim Weber's meeting with Berkshire Hathaway board of directors, 116
    (*see also* Berkshire Hathaway)
Burger King, 26
Burke–Gilman Trail, 99, 100

Callaway, 60
Cambridge Analytica, 180
cancer, 163–173
    aftermath for Jim Weber, 177–178
    consequences of treatment for Jim
        Weber, 175–177
    and Jim Weber's attempts to return
        to running after treatment, 174
    Jim Weber's return to work after
        treatment, 173–174
Caprara, Carson, 78–80, 86, 92
captured companies, 111
carbon neutrality, 185
Carlson, Katie, 139
Carlson School of Management
    (University of Minnesota), 69–70
Carrozza, Paul, 58
Cascadia (Brooks shoe), 54, 76
Castleman, Peter, 38
Catholic Church, 180
Cavens, Darrell, 120, 152–153, 156
Charting Brooks's Future plan,
    143–147, 152
cheating, 180
Chicago Marathon, 56, 91–92
Chili's, 26–27
circle of competence, at Berkshire,
    123
climate change, 184–185
Coleman Company, 30–35, 111
Coleman Spas, 31–34
collateralized debt obligations
    (CDOs), 75
Collins, Jim, 78
computers, 18–19
Connect Leadership Development
    Training Program, 139
consolidation, 190
consumer focus, 127–129
conventional wisdom, going against,
    49–50
Converse, 57
corporate culture (see culture)
Corporate Equality Index (Human
    Rights Campaign), 186

corporate governance, at Berkshire,
    118–120
corporate raiders, 24–25
COVID-19 pandemic (2020–),
    156–161, 183–184, 195
Cowles Media Company, 19–20
Cray Research, 15
culture:
    at Berkshire, 123
    at Brooks, 51
    maintaining during challenging
        times, 136–139
    measuring cultural strength,
        139–141
    need for greater integration and
        alignment, 144–147
Cunningham, Lawrence A., 106
curiosity, authentic leadership and,
    70–71
customer focus, 148f

Dain Bosworth, 15
data, from runners, 200
Dick's Sporting Goods, 51, 186
digital shopping, 133–136
Dillard's, 51
Dimon, Jamie, 169
distribution:
    Brooks's multichannel strategy, 197
    choices led by Brooks's runner
        focus, 47–50, 52f
    construction of Midwest
        distribution center, 153–155
diversity, 186–187
DNA midsole technology, 90–91
Dodge, Matt, 158
Drexel Burnham, 24
Duncan, Liz, 204
Dylan, Bob, 107

e-commerce, 133–136
economic stimulus package (2020),
    189–190
Edelman Trust Barometer, 181
Eder, Larry, 56

Editor's Choice Award *(Runner's World)*, 87
Election Day (2020), as paid holiday, 187
Ellwein, Mike, 31
empathy, authentic leadership and, 71
empowered culture, at Berkshire, 123
"Empower Her" collection, 186
Enron, 122
esophagectomy, 165

Facebook, 180
family footwear, 45, 60
Fauci, Anthony, 199
Federal Reserve, 75, 189
Finish Line, 51
Fleet Feet, 48–49
Float and Feel, 80
FLOEEAT, 145–147
Floyd, George, 161, 186
focus, authentic leadership and, 70
Foot Locker, 42, 51
Frankl, Viktor, 167
Friedman, Milton, 108
Fruit of the Loom:
    and Berkshire Hathaway's Russell Athletic acquisition, 57, 105–106, 113
    Brooks and, 86, 111
    Warren Buffet's proposal to make Brooks independent of, 106, 120
Fulton, Mr. (math teacher), 7
Furrer, Amanda, 87

Gas Works Park (Seattle), 100
Gebrselassie, Haile, 73
Gel (Asics shoe), 42
Generation Y, 127
Ghost (Brooks shoe), 54, 60, 87, 185
GLIDE, 115
global disruptions, navigating, 143–162
Glycerin (Brooks shoe), 54
graduate school, 17–18
Grand Metropolitan, 30

Great Recession (2008), 73–75, 127–129
Gretzky, Walter, 127
The Grinch Who Stole Christmas (Seuss), 195
Grunewald, Gabe, 163–164, 174
Guyman, Charlotte, 119, 120, 168–170

Häagen-Dazs, 28–29
Hill-Murray School (Maplewood, Minn.), 8–10, 17, 23
Hills, Tamara, 92, 93, 99, 150
hockey, 7–12, 192
Holmes, Elizabeth, 180
Horan, John, 58
Houston Astros, 180
"How Millennials Ended the Running Boom" (*Wall Street Journal* article), 128
Hull, Bobby, 7
Human Rights Campaign Corporate Equality Index, 186
Humphrey, Pete, 65, 78–79, 86
Hunter, Iain, 84–85
Hyperion 2 (Brooks shoe), 157

IBM PC, 18, 19
IDEO, 79–80
"inclusion imperative," 186–187
income inequality, 187–191, 190*f*
industry consolidation, 190
Insights Discovery test, 6
inspiration, as Brooks's purpose, 62–63, 182–184
integration, culture and, 144–147
integrity, 122
Internet, shopping on, 133–136
inventory control, 52–53
investors:
    and Brooks's success, 47, 56–58
    and private capital pools, 110–111
    and private equity, 112
    syncing CEO's strategy with investors' objectives, 106–108

Isakov, Gregory Alan, 172
Iverson, Ann, 38

Jacobs, Regina, 180
James, Chet, 48
James, Laurel, 48
James, LeBron, 57
Janaszak, Steve, 10
J.H. Whitney & Company, 37–40,
    45–46, 112
*Joseph and the Amazing Technicolor
    Dreamcoat* (Webber and Rice),
    109–110
JSC, 153
Jurek, Scott, 54, 76

Kellogg's, 29
Kerr, Josh, 203
Klobuchar, Amy, 191
Knight, Phil, 57
Knox, Beth, 150

Larson, Dave, 56, 90
leadership, authenticity and (*see*
    authenticity)
leadership manifesto, 38–40
Leo Burnett Worldwide, 30
Levin, 28
Levin, Jerry, 24–26, 31, 34
Lewis, Michael, 183
Linden, Des, 147–150, *149,* 157, 174
Lotus 1-2-3, 19
Lotus Symphony, 19
Lululemon, 60

Mackey, Danny, 203
Macy's, 51
Man's Search for Meaning (Frankl), 167
marketing:
    and 2012 Olympic Team Trials,
        96–98
    during COVID pandemic, 160–161
    creative efforts at Brooks, 55–56
    digital shopping, 133–136
    at Pillsbury, 30

Marvin Windows, 15
MBA, 17–18
McDougall, Christopher, 75–76
McGill, Charles, 23–24
McGrath, Mrs. (English teacher), 7
Mead, Margaret, 78
Meeting de Montreuil, 203
Meyer, Greg, *44*
Milken, Michael, 24
millennials:
    and bust of second running boom,
        125–129
    and digital shopping, 133–136
minimalist design, 79, 86
mission statement, 61
moats:
    at Brooks, 39, 40, 58
    Warren Buffet on importance of,
        120–121
    defined, 28
Mueller, Holger, 153–154
Munger, Charlie, 58, 70, 106, 118, 122
Music City Track Carnival
    (Nashville), 203

Napier, George, 36
Natural Habitat Joint Motion
    (NHJM), 84
Nautilus, Inc., 38
net promoter scores (NPS), 138–139
New Balance, 30, 42, 43, 89
New England Patriots, 180
New York Times, 92, 99
Nike:
    Brooks and, 62, 133
    and Brooks's competitive
        environment, 28, 30, 37–38, 42,
        43, 114, 129
    endorsement successes, 57
    marketing, 56
    and Olympic Team Trials (2012),
        96–98
    statement products in 1970s, 60
Nike Pegasus shoe, 50
Nordstrom, 51

North Face, 60
North Star, defining a, 61–65
Norwest Bank, 16–18, 108
Novogratz, Jacqueline, 192

O'Brien, Herb, 35
O'Brien International, 35–36, 59
Olympic Games (Beijing, 2008), 73
Olympic Games (Tokyo, 2020), 203
Olympic marathon trials (2020), 157
Olympic Team Trials (2012), 84–85, 96–98, *97*
Operation Warp Speed, 184
Oppenheimer, Deanna, 120
Overlake Hospital (Bellevue, Washington), 164–165

pandemic (2020–), 156–161, 183–184, 195
PCs (personal computers), 18–19
Pellegrini, Carlos A., 177–178
Peloton, 60
Pentland Sports, 65, 78
performance, as timeless, 125–141
performance technology, 132–133
Perlman, Ron, 31
permanence, at Berkshire, 123–124
Pillsbury, 23–31, 38, 109, 190
Pillsbury Doughboy, 27–30
Pillsbury Hungry Jack Biscuits, 27–30
The PIMS (Profit Impact of Marketing Strategy) Principles (Buzzell and Gale), 27
Piper Jaffray, 38
Plank, Kevin, 129
playbook for integration/alignment at Brooks, 144–147–147
Pons de Vier, Patrick, 130–131, 143
portable spa industry, 32–33 (*see also* Coleman Spas)
positioning (*see* brand positioning)
praise, importance at Berkshire, 123
Prefontaine, Steve, 96
The Premonition (Lewis), 183
Prince, 60

private capital pools, 110–111
private equity, 31, 37–38, 59, 112–113
Pryor, Chris, 10
public companies, tyranny of quarterly earnings at, 109–110
public health:
    active lifestyle and, 182–184
    income inequality and sports participation, 188
PureProject footware collection, 86, 115
purpose, mission versus, 61

quality control, 50
quarterly earnings, tyranny of, 109–110
Queensland marathon, 203

racism, 161–162
Rave Run (*Runner's World* feature), 14
Raynor, Tom, 48–49
recession (1982), 16
"Recover to Run" plan, 158
recycled/renewable materials, 201
Redhook Brewery, 99
Reebok, 42
renewable energy/materials, 201
research-driven design, 80–84
return on investment (ROI) flywheel, 40
Revel (Brooks shoe), 143
Revlon Company, 31
risk management, at Berkshire, 122
Road Runner Sports, 50–51
Rockey, Helen, 38, 45–46
Rock 'n' Roll Marathon, 89–90
Rohosy, Anne, 120
Ross, Tom, 115
Rudow, Martin, 54–55
Ruegger, Silvia, 166
Run Happy, 87–98
    as billion dollar idea, 92–96
    bringing the ethos to runners, 89–92
    and Chicago Marathon, 56

defining, 87–89
elements of, 88*f*–89*f*
as goal at Brooks, 196
and Olympic Team Trials (2012),
    96–98, *97*
and Jim Weber's meeting with
    Berkshire board of directors, 117
Runner's World:
awards for Adrenaline GTS 4, 54
and Brooks 100th anniversary
    celebration, 100–101
and Brooks's upward swing, 58
on Ghost shoe, 87
Rave Run feature, 14
survey on runners' shoe buying
    habits, 51
survey on shoe attributes most
    important to runners, 48
Running Industry Diversity Coalition
    (RIDC), 186–187
Running Network, 54
Run Sights Lab, 159–160, 199
Run Signature philosophy, 84–87, 92,
    93, 98
RunTex, 58, 78
Runtopia, 130
Russell Athletic, 57–58, 106, 111, 113
Russell Group, 106

St. Cloud State University, 11
St. Paul Civic Center, 7–8
Salomon–Amer Sports, 130
Saucony, 42
scaling, 151–156
Schaefer family, 6
Scheffy, Clark, 156
Schultz, Hannah, 175
Seattle, Washington:
    new Brooks headquarters, 99–100
    Jim Weber's first trip to, 34–35
self-defined runners (SDRs), 126
Sell, Brian, 73
Shank, John, 29
Sheridan, Dan, 136, 154, 174
shipping time, 53

Shorter, Frank, 125
Shox (Nike shoe), 42
Sigma Nu Fraternity, 15
Sims, Tom, 36–37
Sims Sports, 36–37, 59, 110–112
snowboarding, 36–37
"The Social Responsibility of
    Business Is to Increase Its
    Profits" (Friedman), 108
Special Olympics USA Games (2018),
    150–151
specialty running stores, 48–53, 80
Spoor, Bill, 25–29
Sporting Goods Intelligence, 58
Sports Authority, 134
sports participation, income
    inequality and, 188
spreadsheets, 18–19
stability shoes, 53
Steak and Ale (Bennigan's), 25
Stumptown Twilight Meet, 203
subprime mortgage crisis, 75
Super Jock 'n Jill, 48
Supplier Code of Conduct and
    Responsible Sourcing Standards,
    185
supply chain optimization (SCO),
    153–154
sustainability, 201
Switzer, Kathrine, 43
systemic racism, 161–162

takeovers, 30
Tarahumara people, 76
Target, 15
Taylor, Breonna, 161
Theranos, 180
3M, 15
Thurston, Robin, 120
Title IX, 43
Troubled Asset Relief Program
    (TARP), 75
trust, 179–192
    and authentic leadership, 71
    of customers, 54–56

trust (*cont.*)
  filling the white space as a
    business, 181–182
Tuck School of Business (Dartmouth
    College), 17–24, 190
tuned ride, 200
Twin Cities Marathon (1982), 13–14
Tycoon (computer simulation
    game), 20–21

Under Armour, 129
University of Minnesota, 11–12,
    15–16, 69–70
University of Washington Dawg Dash
    10K, 164
USA Track & Field, 96
US Bank, 16

value creation flywheel, 39*f*
Vantage (Brooks shoe line), 131
Vibram "five fingers" shoe, 76, 78
Vietnam, as manufacturing site, 130
Vigano, Paul, 38, 40
VisiCalc, 18
Volkswagen, 180

"wall of bricks" analogy, 45–47
Wall Street, 74–75, 109
Wall Street Journal, 26, 127–128
Ward, Jack, 57
Washington Medical center, 177–178
wealth inequality, 190
wear testing, 50
Weber, Declan, 166
Weber, Jim:
  appointment as Brooks's CEO, 46
  at Brooks (*see* Brooks Running)
  building credentials for business
    leadership, 15–18
  at business school, 16–22
  cancer aftermath, 177–178
  cancer onset and diagnosis, 163–173
  cancer treatment, 170–173
  childhood, 3–11

at Coleman, 30–35
college, 11–16
consequences of cancer treatment,
    175–177
discovery of running, 12–15
hockey, 6–12
marriage, 16
in MBA program, 17–18
at O'Brien International, 35–36
Omaha meeting with Warren
    Buffett, 113–115
open letter to the running
    community, 81–82
personal leadership manifesto, 66–
    69, 71–72
at Pillsbury, 23–30
at Sims Sports, 36–37
Weber, Joel, 17, 21, 166
Weber, Kacey, 166
Weber, Lennon, 166
Weber, Marisa, 166
Weber, MaryEllen:
  marriage, 16
  at St. Cloud, 11
  and Jim Weber's cancer, 164, 166,
    171, 172
  and Jim Weber's early running
    experiences, 12
Weber, Michael, 17, 166
Weber, Reid, 35, 166, 172
Weber, Teagan, 166
Weber's Supper Club, 5–6
Wells Fargo, 180
Whitney, Wheelock, 15–16, 29
Whitney & Company (*see* J.H.
    Whitney & Company)
Wilhelm, Rick, 96, 98
Willey, David, 100–101
Williams, Jesse, 96, 98
women, Brooks's competitive
    environment and, 43

Zuckerberg, Mark, 115
Zulily, 152

ABOUT THE AUTHOR

In seventh grade at a Minnesota middle school, Jim Weber dreamed of being either a professional hockey player or a CEO when he grew up. After hanging up his skates in college, Weber became a CEO for the first time at age thirty, finding his love for leading people, growing brands, and creating successful businesses.

Weber joined Brooks Running Company as CEO in 2001 and is credited for the Seattle-based company's aggressive turnaround, focusing the team solely on delivering personally inspiring products and experiences that keep people running. The business and brand success caught the attention of Warren Buffett, who declared Brooks a standalone subsidiary company of Berkshire Hathaway Inc. in 2012. Ernst & Young awarded Weber "Entrepreneur of the Year" in the Pacific Northwest region in 2013, and *Runner's World* in 2015 named him one of the most influential innovators in the running industry.

Weber's professional journey includes leadership roles for several consumer product brands, such as chairman and CEO of Sims Sports, president of O'Brien International, vice president of The Coleman Company, and various roles with The Pillsbury Company. Weber also spent several years in banking as managing director of U.S. Bancorp Piper Jaffray Seattle Investment Banking practice and as a commercial banking officer at Norwest Bank Minneapolis (now Wells Fargo).

Weber received a bachelor's degree from the University of Minnesota's Carlson School of Management and a master of business administration with high distinction from the Tuck

School of Business at Dartmouth College. He currently serves on the boards of directors for Brooks and the Tuck School, and resides just outside Seattle with his wife, MaryEllen, who first caught his attention on the ice during high school.